The French at Home

The French at Home

A Nation's Character, Culture and Genius as
Observed by an American Diplomat

Albert Rhodes

Edited by Paul Dennis Sporer

ROLLRIGHT BOOKS

Anza Publishing, Chester, NY 10918
Rollright Books is an imprint of Anza Publishing
Copyright © 2005 by Anza Publishing

This work is a new, unabridged edition of *The French at Home,*
by Albert Rhodes, originally published in 1875.

Library of Congress Cataloging-in-Publication Data
Rhodes, Albert, b. 1840.
  The French at home / Albert Rhodes ; edited by Paul Dennis
Sporer.-- New, unabridged ed.
    p. cm.
  Originally published: 1875.
  Includes index.
  ISBN 1-932490-38-8 (hardcover : alk. paper)
  1. France–Social life and customs–19th century.
  2. National characteristics, French.
  I. Sporer, Paul D. II. Title.

DC33.R47 2005
944.06--dc22   2005015558

Visit AnzaPublishing.com for more information on outstanding
authors and titles. Please support our efforts to restore great
literature to a place of prominence in our culture.

∞ This book is printed on acid-free paper.

ISBN: 1-932490-38-8 (hardcover)
ISBN: 1-932490-56-6 (softcover)

Contents

Editor's Preface

Albert Rhodes was born in Pittsburgh, Pennsylvania in 1840. He held many important government positions representing America abroad. During the administration of President Johnson, he was United States consul at Jerusalem, and under President Grant, he was consul at Rotterdam and charge d'affaires at the Hague. He was also consul at Rouen, France, and at Elberfeld, Germany, from 1877 to 1885. Rhodes frequently contributed to American, French, and British periodicals, largely on the characteristics of life and people on the European continent.

An earlier work of his was *The French at Home,* originally published by the New York firm of Dodd & Mead in 1875. French culture, taste, politeness, cookery, art, and desire for military glory, are all keenly observed by someone who had a lengthy foreign residence in the consular and diplomatic service. Rhodes not only describes the many activities he witnessed on the streets and in the homes of ordinary people, but he also attempts to look deeply into the French character, into a nation's "personality", to perceive what makes them better or worse than Americans. The results of his observations are presented here in a form that could be considered both brilliant and instructive.

We have been faithful to the original text in the areas of spelling, punctuation and grammar. It is interesting to note how many French terms have changed in meaning and usage since the time the book was written. We have added an index, which contains many phrases and expressions from the text.

PAUL DENNIS SPORER

CHAPTER I

Character

THE EARLY GAUL is reputed stalwart and of good height, and his posterity resembles him except in stature. The great battles of Louis the Fourteenth and Napoleon, it is believed, have done something toward lowering the French stature, both in the suffering to which the population was subjected, and the indifferent character of progenitors left behind the armies through constitutional disabilities. This, however, is a theory difficult of demonstration.

The physical characteristics of the present race show, in comparison with the American, a frame more compact, limbs rounder, and stature smaller. The lines of formation in the extremities are more graceful, especially at the point where the wrist and ankle enter the hand and foot. The lean, lanky person common in America is rare in this race. But the type of a large class of Englishmen offers a greater contrast, — he of the long neck, exposed teeth, long, thin ankles with bony projections, the calves well up under the hinges of the knee, large feet and hands, and frowzy complexion; a portraiture in France which is made the scapegoat of British eccentricity.

Compared to the Frenchman, the American is more loosely hung together, and has more swing and give in gait and gesture. A Frenchman cannot sprawl. An American does it with facility, over chairs, counters, or dry-goods boxes. In their repose there is the difference between the Dorking fowl which perches in the sun, and the Shanghai who basks his loose limbs in a royal spread.

Out-of-door exercises of a rough kind, such as steeple-chasing, yachting, and pedestrianism, do not enter into the Frenchman's habits. He does no hard trained rowing, but plays with his oars as a pretext for donning a fantastic costume, and repairing to Asnières or Bougival in pleasure junketings. He and the water, fresh or salt, do not seem to be made for each other. He takes a swimming-master as he does a dancing-master, — to learn. One of the establishments which line the Seine is the scene of his first efforts, where he is suspended in the water by a rope, held by the *maître de natation* overhead, who, as he walks slowly along holding the pupil up, encourages him in the style of a fencing-master, with words such as, "Voyons là-bas, un peu de courage. Êtes-vous prêt? C'est bien, partons—un, deux—un, deux" — marking the time with his feet to the "one, two," with an ardor interesting to a transatlantic spectator. On the seashore the venturesome swimmers are generally English or Americans. It is the same with boating. The Frenchman usually contents himself with sitting on the beach, looking out on the sea, while the other two nationalities must be in or of it.

The national exercise is fencing, on which much time and application is bestowed, both as a matter of hygiene and a means of defending that honor about which there is so much ado. Single-stick and foot-ball come next. There are repulsive features in boxing which have always prevented it from taking root on French soil. Public wrestling is in vogue. There is something classic in this, which appeals to the Athenian-Frenchman's love of art, and it is patronized by high and low. Kicking is practised as a science,—standing, and on the back, — particularly by the lower class. There is no running or jumping to speak of, of any kind. They excel in fencing, football, and wrestling, but are behind English and Americans in other athletic sports. In the easy parade riding about the Bois, they are, perhaps, more graceful than others, but not as firmly seated. Some of them could hardly keep their saddles in a rough ride across country. In this, as in many other things, utility gives way to the ornamental. A horse trained to climb, arch his neck, and show riding-school paces, bestrode by a cavalier who sits easily and bows gracefully, is the usual limit of aspiration in the way of horsemanship. Comanche and Mexican riding, if seen, would be regarded as miraculous. When American circus-riders first turned summersaults on barebacked horses in Paris, it was too much for the nerves of the public: they cried, "Assez, assez!"

Indoors the national game is dominoes. The habitué of a second-class café has his pipe in a rack of the place of his choice, and is of routine attendance. Smoking *caporal* and drinking beer are accessories to the game. There is more billiard-playing than with us. They excel in their carom game, and regard pocketing balls as a shameful business, much as we look upon the *rolly-bolly* of urchins,—in a word, unworthy of an adult. The monotony of this café life to an active American is tiring,—the eternal rattling of bones under a cloud of smoke, irritating.

The Bible-taught Anglo-American sees something in the Frenchman which displeases him. If he is of theological austerity, it shocks him. He charges him with wickedness,—absence of moral sense. The Gaul replies, that religion is a matter of education, and that the Bible must not be confounded with a perfect code of morals, as they are two distinct things, one being an incomplete expression of the other; that the Bible worshipper endeavors to create an artificial moral man instead of educating a natural one; and the Frenchman puts himself forward as the moral man whose nature has not been warped or thwarted in its growth. He claims, too, to be more advanced, and predicts that fifty years hence we shall be standing where he does now. Such language, of course, has but little weight in transatlantic estimation, and he continues to be arraigned for laxity of morals.

But what is puzzling to the austere theologue is, that there are certain clustering qualities of symmetrical harmony and goodness found in the character of the Gaul, which are not the development of an evil, but a virtuous nature. The key to this apparently paradoxical state is to be found in the man's love of the beautiful with which he strives to invest his religion and his life. He is the cultivated pagan of the nineteenth century, whose faculties are developed in a school of aesthetics where even his acknowledged church is made subordinate, notwithstanding its prestige and requirements. The beautiful in art, in nature, in the soul and physical form, is the idea of which he is possessed; and when this is borne in mind it is easier to understand and judge him.

The Frenchman has his share of vanity. One of the forms of it is his ambition to wear a bit of red ribbon, for which he sometimes sacrifices his own esteem. Proud of himself and his country, which he calls *"la grande nation,"* the scream of the American eagle is not worse than this. This vanity is the cause of part of his ignorance. It is common among journalists and publicists of Paris to write of their countrymen as the wittiest, politest, best instructed, and most civilized people of the world, — reiterated from day to day with conviction of truth. This is done with scanty knowledge of other countries; for the French, as a rule, know less of other peoples than any of the other enlightened nations,— a knowledge which is naturally indispensable to a just comparison. They are, in this respect, the Chinese of the West. The centre of the world and all its excellences are to be found within the line which maps out France: beyond that is barbarian waste.

The Frenchman's education, from an American point of view, is defective in what relates to geography and history of nations other than his own. The educated Frenchman will be found to possess a fair knowledge of the classics (with an excellent pronunciation), of mathematics, science, and art generally, and of the literature and history of his own country. An ordinary American lad would put him to the blush on a question of foreign history or geography. It might be affirmed in his presence, without much fear of contradiction, that Birkenhead was in Ireland, and Missouri formed part of the Mexican Republic.

Such is his national pride, that he is apt to believe that all foreigners regret that they are not Frenchmen. His Chauvinism has nothing analogous in modern history. In its sincerity, there is nothing like it this side of biblical days, when the Jews believed themselves chosen of God. According to him, he is of the elect vanguard of civilization, which overcomes obstacles and shows the way to others. His country is the birthplace of noble political conception, and the cradle of every art. It is the battle-ground where truth is vindicated and error is crushed. From it go out enduring principles of liberty and justice, which carry deliverance with them wherever they are promulgated. Of these things the typical Frenchman has little doubt. In his entirety, he is a man standing on a summit, holding in his hand the torch of enlightenment and progress, whose beneficent rays are thrown broadcast over less favored peoples until they reach the darkest corners of the earth, for which they never can be sufficiently grateful. But— and the but is terrible — he cannot himself profit by the light which he so freely gives to others.

In some of this there is truth, but in his Chauvinistic hands it assumes an exaggerated form.

In the midst of his inconstancies, he is constant in his worship of a theoretical liberty, designated by his severest critics as Utopian. He may renounce it a dozen times under discouragement, for he is easily discouraged, but he comes back to it as the needle points to the pole. He fumes, harangues, and sheds his blood for this pet idea, until the fruits of victory are almost within his grasp, when he finds at the last moment, to use his own words, that he has been betrayed. According to his explanation, the plan is always perfect, but the men are found wanting, in being too weak or too strong, too corrupt, or not of sufficient elasticity for a political crisis. And thus the same story is enacted from father to son.

His history has been a pursuit of liberty, and it has always eluded him like an *ignis fatuus*. Today he is a revolutionist, resisting tyranny to the death in the name of freedom; and tomorrow, as soon as he holds the reins of power, in turn becomes as much a tyrant as he whom he has overthrown. Yet he is always a votary of liberty. Like the thoughtless child brooking no restraint, who, seizing the butterfly which he admires, destroys its beauty, so the Frenchman kills liberty as soon as it is in his power; and this from being so entirely convinced of the perfection of his own theories that he regards opposition to them as wilful perversity, and he proceeds to convert those holding adverse opinions at the point of the bayonet. And thus he goes on until the position of the bayonet is reversed, for, as a German prince has said, "You can do almost anything with bayonets except sit on them."

Thus he is intolerant in governing, and turbulent when governed. His thought is bold, but his action is feeble. He has long torpors and terrible awakenings, when he wishes to do everything at once. He does not respect the law as much as he does its agents. Law is more or less abstract; but the agents are palpable, and their livery and surroundings appeal to his pronounced sense of the theatrical.

He is warm-hearted and confiding, but with little reverence for men or things. In the zenith of the reign of Napoleon III. there was no loyalty for him such as that which exists for Queen Victoria of England. The motives of the best leaders are often questioned in France. Cincinnatus himself would not be long above suspicion, to say nothing of his simplicity of character, with which France could never be governed. There must be the *panache*, the blare of trumpets, and the gold lace, with those eternal phrases which have always enraptured the ear of the nation, "Quarante siècles vous contemplent," "L'empire, c'est la paix," and the rest of it. He is a lounger. The sight of a procession of any kind gives him great pleasure, but a martial one with its shrill trumpets plunges him into ecstasy. The slightest ripple of excitement draws this *badaud*. A crowd gathers on the Pont Neuf, looking intently down into the Seine. New-comers elbow their way to the parapet. The spectators are interested in what is transpiring below; and the thought flashes through the mind, that there is a man over-board or drowning. What is it? Pierre has caught a fish three inches long!

He is constantly complaining of his government, whatever it is, as if each nation does not have as good a government as it deserves, — as if it depended on the government alone to correct abuses. He accuses the administration of doing too much, and with reason; but he does not attempt to do anything himself. He is taken charge of, bag and baggage, by the government on his travels, and carefully looked after in his domicile as if he were a child. Even the omnibus conductor in a certain measure takes him under his protection, demands his fare with an air of command, and sets him down at his destination as if he were a parcel. The man clothed in government authority assumes that laconic, not-to-be-questioned air, which we frequently see in our naval or army officers on duty. This official starch pervades more particularly the subordinate agents of each branch of the government. The private citizen is always inclining himself politely right and left; the official is oppressed with a sense of his dignity, and seems to say, "Don't trifle with me, for I have a terrible responsibility on my shoulders."

The Frenchman has ardent longings for liberty which excite American sympathy, but he has no patience. The past seems to show that he is happiest under a strong governor, but this he systematically denies. Few of them can be trusted with power. Ambition turns their heads, and leads them to extremes and oppression; then society's sub-strata heave, and hurl them from their places. The love of parade is ingrained, and theatrical effects disturb their reason. A well-contrived dramatic *coup* in politics elicits their admiration in spite of the iniquity of the thing. In a word, they are artists to the point of losing moral discernment, — from the minister to the barber, from the painter to the cook.

Yet few understand liberty in theory better than they. They discuss it from a higher standpoint than we, show a thorough appreciation of its advantages, then make a hurried, nervous effort to put their theories into practice, and, not meeting with immediate success, sit down in a fit of discouragement until one strong man gets hold of the reins again; then it is too late. They make the fatal mistake of making their republic before they make their republicans.

The charge of deceit and falseness sometimes urged against the Frenchman is, of course, the result of *extreme politeness*. He treats his fellows with courtesy by system. The Anglo-Saxon is impressed by his especial marks of interest, and he judges the Gaul by himself. He knows that if he were "enchanted" to see and "desolated" to quit a fellow-creature, that man would be a friend for whom he would stand ready to make sacrifices. Thus, after an effusive reception from the Frenchman, the man from over the Channel or Atlantic is disgusted when his mercurial friend can hardly recall his name or face the next time he meets him. Yet the Gaul's intentions are of the best, and more or less philosophical. He tries to get the most out of life, by making it smooth and pleasant all round. He endeavors to cast sunshine into the five or ten minute halts along life's journey. Out of peer and prolétaire he has his tribute of happiness, for no reasonable person can resist him; and he tries to give as good as he gets, thus establishing that system of exchange which makes of the French the attractive people that they are. When thrown for a few minutes with an unthawable creature, he will not make the attempt to be amiable; and here he is right again, for life is too short to melt the ice with which such a one is incrusted. In this case he wraps himself in pleasant souvenirs, and draws on the past for the present.

Life is compelled to yield all that it has to give. Every function of man's nature is made to contribute to his enjoyment, and thus his sensuous life is larger than ours. This sybarite makes requisitions upon the five senses to their full capacity, and thus enriches his existence, where with us it is often meagre. Material life is studied and made a familiar science. In the matter of eating, it is carried to a perfection not given to every foreigner to appreciate, and this has its effect upon character. Absence of dyspepsia or any malady of the stomach, nourishing food, easy digestion, good climate, and the best wine in the world, make of them a comparatively happy people. The presiding genius of every kitchen is hygiene, which never tolerates such disturbers of the stomach's repose, for instance, as hot rolls and buckwheat cakes. Some of their greatest men have not thought it beneath their dignity to study the pleasures of the palate. Alexandre Dumas and Brillat-Savarin were frequently in the habit of cooking for their guests, and the latter wrote a book on the subject which in point of style is nearly equal to Madame de Sévigné's; and what between the literary excellence of the book, and the good things of this world whereof it treats, one's mouth is made to water in its perusal. A palate and stomach corrupted by hot corn-bread and saleratus biscuit do not at once take kindly to Gallic nourishment, and sometimes never. It is not encouraging to the American reformers of abuse in food and drink to have a Texan say, after a dinner at the Trois Frères, that he prefers the pork and corn-dodger of his native State, or that he never wants to eat a better dinner than that he has in the Palais Royal for two francs, including a half bottle of "the best kind of wine." One can fancy the effect of such statements on Frenchmen, the shrug and smile of commiseration. I was once at a small dinner party in Paris at a restaurant famed for its wine-cellar, where a bottle of Château Margaux was

poured, and one of the convives, through inadvertence or ignorance, raised the decanter to water his glass, when an old *garçon*
standing behind him stayed his arm, saying solemnly, "If you put
water in that wine, God will never forgive you."

Like all people with subtle, impulsive organizations, his capacity for suffering is equal to that for enjoying. He cannot remain
moody and depressed any length of time, as the Anglo-Saxon can.
While the latter begins to contemplate suicide, he has already
thrown himself from a Seine bridge or the Vendôme Column. The
calm, equable happiness of a heavy nature, which never rises to
his heights of keen enjoyment, nor descends to the depths of his
poignant suffering, he cannot understand. He is always on the
crest of life's wave or in its trough. The Teutonic medium, never
completely at the bottom or the top, is not for him. His brain fibre
is too fine for that.

The central point of interest to the young men who make pretensions to elegance is the Jockey Club, where one of the requi-
sites of membership is a certain income. Imitation of the Englishman is in vogue in this society, and it is an interesting spectacle
to see one of these young gentlemen affecting his ways. In public
he discards his nourishing and toothsome Bordeaux for pale ale
at dinner, and washes down his cold beef with decoctions of weak
tea at breakfast. He has been educated to take tea only in case of
sickness, and when he declares a preference for it the truth of his
statement may reasonably be doubted. He cannot acquire the
English language in spite of fits of assiduity in that direction, but
learns a few words considered indispensable to every member of
his circle. He pities him who says *club* (French sound of *u),* which
he ostentatiously pronounces *kleub*. He may achieve beef, but in
moments of forgetfulness he says *bif.* To shake hands is considered an English custom, and he frequently joins the word *shek-
and* to the action. He is responsible for several ill-assorted marriages between English and French words, such as *boule-dog* and

black-bouler, and is the author of such hideous hybrids as *dogue-car* and *monde-sportique.* On meeting an American or an English-man, he makes a heavy draft on his knowledge of the language, and turns off several words with expansion, becomes bankrupt, and goes into liquidation in his own tongue.

The *ut de poitrine* of all Frenchmen is, of course, the *th.* These vexatious consonants, according to tradition, have driven several of them to self-destruction. When it is proposed to repeat such phrases as "thirty thousand thrushes thronging through the thicket," one can imagine the heavy demand made on the last letter of the alphabet.

The young men set in fashion's mould are generally garbed in the English cut, a trifle modified where the lines are hard, — a natural result of their finer sense of art. They are an improvement in manner, if not in dress, on their neighbors across the Channel. In affecting English ways, which came in with the horse-race, they have, however, lost some of their good-breeding as compared with their seniors who are passing away. There is a suavity about the elders which they do not possess. Young France does not hold his hat under his arm while talking to a lady at the side of a carriage or at the door of a dwelling. He raises his hat, and gives the swoop, but replaces it directly. His elder is capable of exposing his bald head to the sun several minutes, unless commanded to cover. His compliments are better turned and more insinuating. To western eyes his gallantry borders upon extravagance; but there is a French axiom that it is impossible to be too polite, and this bears him out in the estimation of his countrymen.

In the upper classes of most countries, foreign servants are employed to keep up knowledge of a foreign language, or have it imparted to children, as well as to comply with the requirements of a certain vogue. In America they are French, in England, German (in imitation of the royal family Germanized through marriages), and in France, English. In large establishments it is

not unusual to see the service composed entirely of the h-drop-
pers, who are employed because they speak the language of
Shakespeare.

The small number, however, of those who admire British manners and customs, is lost in the rank and file of French society.
The nation is as strong now in its Gallic elements as when conquered by Caesar; and the young men who exercise an influence
in the general movement of things are very different from the
elegant nullities who act and try to talk after the British pattern.

As to the woman of France, her coquetry is proverbial. It is the
oil in the salad. A Spanish proverb has it that a kiss without a
mustache is like an egg without salt; and the Frenchman avers
that a woman without a certain degree of coquetry is like a
saltless soup.

The woman of rigid principles and adamantine virtue is everywhere held up for popular admiration, and men say they admire
her; and they *do* in a lukewarm fashion, but this is equivalent to
the faint praise which damns. They give an intellectual assent to
her claims for superiority, and secretly vote her tame. But for her
whose character is flavored with a trifle of coquetry they stand
ready to commit those acts of folly which are known to be so
pleasing to the gentle sex. Frenchmen affirm that coquetry is a
virtue, and the mother of cleanliness, grace, adornment, and the
desire to please. When it is found in bad company, such as frivolity, dissipation, extravagance, and the like, it may be presumed
that there is too much salt in the soup.

Perhaps the greatest difference between the American and the
French woman is in the voice. That of the former is pitched in a
high key, is thin, often metallic, and rises at times almost to a
shriek. The Gallic woman's has more volume, is sympathetic and
deeper. A harmonious tone in conversation is cultivated, and
there are gentle vibrations in the *timbre,* which exert a magnetic
influence where there is a desire to please. It is powerful in

declamation, as in the mouth of a Rachel, and soft and winning in the quiet of private life. It is a head-voice in America; in France it is from the chest. The nasal sounds, unlike those of New England, come up vibrating from the chest and throat with strong support from the mouth, and thus modified are free from the undignified and discordant twang of the eastern coast.

The face of the American woman is more beautiful than that of any other country. It has delicacy of coloring and feature, and finesse and intellectuality in expression; but the body supporting the head, regarded from an artistic and hygienic point of view, is inferior. For breathing and digesting, the upper part is lacking in depth. In a word, the American is more fragile she is hardly a Diana, and the French is something more, although not the Hebe of Rubens.

The French woman's face is as handsome as that of any other in Europe, and fades more slowly. At forty she glides into an embonpoint with an unwrinkled face and a good complexion, — at the age when the English woman becomes heavy-necked and frowzy, and the American pale and wrinkled. The climate has something to do with this, but doubtless her nourishing food, generous wine, and out-of-door air, much more. Her mode of living contributes thereto, — the exercise and development of each function in a more natural and sensuous manner than with us. There are ascetic ideas in America which have a tendency to retard the physical development of woman; for mind moulds matter. The extremes of American life are unfavorable to a healthy growth, in its fastness as well as its asceticism, where the flesh is corrupted by dissipation, or mortified by certain religious teachings. Aside from these causes is a prevalent notion that it is beneath the dignity of man and woman to occupy themselves with what they shall eat and what they shall drink.

The American has more intellect than her French sister, but the latter has softness where she has pertness. There is nervous excitability and cleverness in one, mellowness and equality of character in the other. The forced, brilliant vitality of woman in America is subject to fits of reaction, for nature has its limit. In the French woman the mind is more even and cheerful, and in the absence of exhaustive and irregular demands made upon it the uniform health is better.

In qualities of a purely mental character, the equal of the American woman cannot, perhaps, be found in the world; but, with all her knowledge and intellectual activity, she lacks that which make the Greeks what they have been, and the French what they are, —organic cultivation. Intwined in these words are taste and art. A riper civilization, though not a purer, shall invest her with a knowledge of these things and a harmony of character not now possessed; and with it will come, alas! that decadence in morals which always marches on the heels of the Beautiful in every age and in every climate. It is sad that such heavy tribute should be exacted as the price of an added enjoyment, but art is inexorable.

The cultivation of the French woman modulates her voice, gives grace of movement in carriage and gesture, and lends a general charm to her person. It imparts that wonderful tact which prevents her from saying a crude or inappropriate thing, and that taste which enables her to say the proper thing at the proper time. In her mouth, a compliment is not an embellished truth, but an unvarnished fact. Her plastic nature receives the impress of those brought in contact with it. She can place herself *en rapport* with the people of all countries, even with those whose character is foreign to her own, and sympathize with the sentiment she meets in those around her. The angular, strong-minded woman does not exist. The French woman can do nothing that renders her repulsive to the other sex. The capable, energetic, speaking woman of America is eccentric and unlovable. The chief end of the French woman's life is to please man; and she cultivates every feminine quality, knowing that what he admires in *her* is to be unlike *him*.

The man-woman in her own country has but little success, and she would have much less in France. Yet the exhibition of talent by woman is not distasteful, so long as there is no violation of the rules of art. The speech and action of the woman of the rostrum, regarded from an artistic point of view, is not lovely to look upon. The French woman may sin against heaven, but not against her *credo* of man-pleasing. She may be faithless to her marriage vows, and send her husband to an untimely grave through her infidelity; but it shall be done with order, and that feminine grace with which she invests all her acts. The winning external appearance is so general, that it is hard to discriminate between the angelic and the *anges déchues.*

What appears to be a plain woman at first sight, at the end of half an hour's conversation often bears the semblance of a handsome woman, when she has deployed her grace of speech and manner, and cajoled her listener with that finesse which belongs to her as if by patent right.

Cultivation, so far as it exists in America, is found only in the higher classes. In France it reaches down to the lower. The shop-girl of the Boulevard, if summoned to wear the coronet of a countess, would do it with the grace of one to whom it belonged by inheritance. In a few hours the chrysalis would disappear so effectually as to lead one to doubt that it ever existed.

And what wonders this grisette does with her slender resources, —what remarkable adaptation of means to ends! The simple tasty hat, and the neat alpaca robe, fitting as well as if made by the celebrity of the Rue de la Paix, are of her construction. Two to one, the tightly drawn immaculate stockings are of her washing. A napoleon, expended in her judicious manner, provides her with a parasol, a pair of well-fitting gloves, and bottines; for well gloved and booted she *will* be, though the heavens should fall. It is given to her sister of no other land to represent so much with so little. From the Batignolles or the heights of Montmartre she daintily descends to her daily occupation with the appearance of one whose life is that of ease and comfort. In the eyry* of the seventh or eighth where she nestles is again presented the struggle between cultivation and poverty. The floor is bare but waxed, and the bed is white. There is the ornamental clock, the crucifix in evergreen, the well-cared-for pot of flowers, and the chirping canary.

Even in the women given over to vice, pagan cultivation redeems it of its most revolting features. Those who haunt the Boulevard of a night in pursuit of their ignoble calling are generally polite, orderly, and well dressed, — in striking contrast to the Anglo-Saxons of the same class as seen in Regent Street. In the romps of the Closerie de Lilas, the grisettes may be wicked, but they are not coarse. In the meretricious twirling and leg-lifting of Mabille, virtue may be thrust out, but there is devotion to art in the bacchantes themselves and their magnificent surroundings.

The French pagan subjects everything to the rules of art. If morality does not appear in harmony with them, it is suppressed. If Virtue robes herself in uncouth garments, she is not tolerated. Vice in the guise of an angel is preferred to goodness which violates the proprieties of art.

Besides, the French mind is naturally sceptical; and the smile concerning the devil, and the lake of fire, has been continually widening since the time of Voltaire. The ferocious and vindictive creature in hoofs and horns has given place to the bon diable who is the first of *blagueurs*. The satanic one has been civilized, patted on the back, and made a good fellow of. He no longer goes about like a roaring lion seeking whom he may devour, but assimilates himself to the spirit of the age, takes his dinners at the wine-renowned Café Anglais, and his coffee at the Café Napolitain, where he philosophically looks on the changing panorama of

---

* Any habitation at a high altitude; also a large nest of an eagle or other bird of prey, typically built high in a tree or on a cliff.

Boulevard life, and contributes his quota of persiflage at its follies. This is a fair portrait of the evil one, done with the Gallic pencil.

Snobbery does not thrive on French soil. Little importance is attached to the manner of living so long as it is not offensive. A man may descend from the aerial heights of a seventh in the Rue Saint Jacques, eat his dinner in a Duval establishment, and enjoy a social position that shall be unquestioned. There are many Rastignacs who thus pass the day in poverty's twilight, and appear at night in the blaze of a salon, in a costume which has cost them the earnings of a year.

Politeness in abundance, but no grovelling. French perspicacity quickly detects where one ends and the other begins. Wonders may be done with the Gaul as long as he is treated to gallant speech and courteous manner. He cannot resist them, for at bottom he is a bon enfant. Stroked the wrong way, he is excitable, unreasonable, and quarrelsome.

Paris suits the lean as well as the full purse. In no great city can one live as cheaply or as extravagantly. There are still *pensions* in existence such as that described in the Père Goriot, in the Rue Lacépèdes and that quarter, where food and lodging with half a bottle of wine a day, and sometimes at discretion, may be had for eighty to ninety francs a month,—sixteen to eighteen dollars. To live in one of these houses is to go back to the last century. With the exception of a few students, they are mostly inhabited by old people with very small incomes, who have no hope of bettering their condition; here and there an ancient countess, a broken baron, an unfortunate tradesman, or what not. They are still within the pale of comparative comfort, for the food and houses are for the most part clean. These terms are at the bottom of the scale for those accustomed to any degree of civilization. Below this, with cheaper rates, come dirt and the man in blouse,—not necessarily, but there are always enough of the unclean to cast a general dirtiness over all. The Siamese twins, poverty and dirt, are to be found in the Faubourg Saint Antoine and Belleville, the cheapest quarters of the great city.

There is an infatuation in the little rentiers about living in the modern Babylon. They could live three times better in the southern provinces with what they spend in Paris, but they cannot be induced to quit the town of their heart. At Tours, situated in a charming country on the banks of the Loire, life is cheaper by half than at Paris. A colony of two or three thousand English, mostly half-pay officers with limited incomes, settled there some time ago, and apparently attained what they sought, — happiness at a moderate price. The Parisian is not bucolic enough to do likewise. An hour or two of Vincennes or Bougival from time to time suffices for him.

At the top of the ladder of expenditure is the splendid life in detached mansions—hotels—in the neighborhood of the Arc de Triomphe, with chateaux on the borders of seas and rivers for the summer months. Next are the spacious apartments, abounding in decorations and mirrors, in the Faubourg Saint Germain, and along the Champs Elysées and its tributaries; after, the modest apartments of the middle classes; then the pinched little entresols and lofty perches of the lean-pursed.

There is a fussy expansiveness in the Frenchman which is ungovernable on grand occasions. The spectacle of an American general in the hour of victory, self restrained and impassible, smoking a cigar, to his eyes must be singular. He, under similar circumstances, would be falling on somebody's neck, and giving himself over to lively transports. Wellington calmly fighting by the watch, and Napoleon nervously taking snuff in great pinches from his waistcoat-pocket, is an illustration of this.

It is not the fashion to repress the expression of feeling in France. When the Anglo-Saxon is of a melting mood, his endeavor is to hide it, and he resorts to blinds, and talks of a cold. If his voice gives way under charged feeling, he explains that it arises from hoarseness, or, in short, any but the true reason. There is nervous apprehension lest any manifestation of it should be observed. In this respect, the Frenchman is everything that he is not. At meeting a friend, his face is radiant with delight, he folds him to his bosom, and kisses him on the cheek; at parting with him for a voyage, he embraces him again, and the unrestrained tear drops from his eyelid. This is done with such natural gracefulness, that it seems a matter of course.

He has dramatic power in voice, expression, and gesture, and uses incisive language, which lends itself to his nature with flexibility. He turns himself inside out before the public. He is always communicating his joys and troubles, and a secret is a heavy burden to him. He almost lives in the open air. When not sleeping or working, he is walking the asphalte, sitting in front of a café, chaired in the Champs Elysées, lounging in the Luxembourg, or pleasure-hunting in suburban forests.

In unrestrained expression of feeling, and wayward pursuit of pleasure, regardless of certain considerations which we deem moral, there is something suggestive of Donatello in his unconsciousness of good and evil before the fatal push from the rock.

A dozen ears may be listening, and he tells Léontine that he loves her; a dozen eyes may be looking, and he embraces her; and the declaration and its accompanying act do not provoke commentary from any of the twelve tongues.

There is a certain shyness about the Englishman in disposing of his food. The Gaul eats in public at his ease, in an open-fronted restaurant, or before it on the common thoroughfare. A scant repast elicits no criticism, and the eater in simple unconsciousness partakes of it as if he were between four walls. He takes his food almost anywhere but where he sleeps. He does not *live* in his lodgings, like his neighbors over the Channel. Out of doors is his home, where he finds his chief comfort and pleasure. If the lid could be taken off Paris on a fine Sunday afternoon, the houses would be found nearly empty; the gayly-dressed inhabitants would be off in wide thoroughfares and parks within the walls, and beyond on grassy slopes and under trees, gathering flowers, listening to music, disporting in the water, kicking the foot-ball, and whirling to the deux temps in sylvan balls.

Sunday in the country is a feature in the programme of Jules, which nothing but bad weather prevents. In these excursions, Léontine is his companion. Six days has she worked in the shop, and the seventh is her holiday, which she enjoys with a zest which a week's work and an early mass impart. With him of her choice she hies* to the woods, by predilection to Robinson, where donkey-riding, swinging, and meandering in the forest are accessories; but the principal feature is dining in that gigantic tree, in whose branches has been cunningly installed a restaurant, with a spiral mount from first to second and third floor. Glee and ardor in the ride, gayety and appetite at the repast, for belles fourchettes are they. In their character of birds perched in the topmost boughs, they sing songs, with accompanying clinks and sallies during the lively partaking. Léontine, blushing with excitement, is handsome to look upon; Jules, gay and gallant, is winning; and yet we must frown upon them and their Sunday-breaking ways.

Looking on this picture of sylvan enjoyment, the guardian of their souls would say, with smiling encouragement, "Right, my children, this is a day of recreation; amuse yourselves, for life is short, and man was created to enjoy." His Calvinistic brother, with stern rebuke, would say, "Sinners, you are breaking the sabbath; you are on the road to everlasting perdition." The spiritual shepherds are indeed wide apart, and continually diverging. Meantime Jules and Léontine amuse themselves to the top of their bent up in the branches of the colossal tree, eating the good things of this world, and drinking bumpers to happiness and long

* To go quickly, or hasten.

life. Little do they perplex themselves about where they are going after the curtain has dropped and the lights are out. They live today; and when questioned about the great tomorrow they reply, "Après nous le deluge!" No self-questionings touching future life, no squaring of present duty with hopes beyond. In contemplating this typical couple, one is unconsciously prompted to look and see if their ears are not furred and pointed like the beautiful animals who knew neither good nor evil.

Mind communicates with mind quickly. A word or speech at a crisis goes through the nation like a flash of electricity. There is a freemasonry extending through all branches of society, in the quick comprehension of significant words, as the "*Jamais*" of Rouher and the "*moblots*" of the people, which become for the time household words of the nation.

There is spontaneous movement in the populace, as where Marie Sass of the opera is called on in the street to sing the old national air, she complying without hesitation, and the crowd taking up the refrain; and where the people daily carry wreaths and flowers, and depose them at the base of a statue of Strasbourg in the Place de la Concorde. An instance of the emotional side of character is furnished in the memorable interview of Bismarck and Jules Favre at the Château de Ferrières, where the latter cannot restrain tears of mortification in presence of the conqueror.

There is one leading trait more characteristic than any other, which no word describes exactly but *blague*. Witty, irrepressible chaffing in daily life is inborn. There is something approximate in the ready humor of the Irishman; but it is less keen and intellectual. In the drawing-room *blague* is toned down into elegant raillery, and in the workshop it takes the hue of broad farce. Its model exponent is the *boulevardier,* who is familiar with passing events, and is an adept in the use of slang and idiom.

Dialect phrases meet one at every corner of Paris, without a knowledge of which the currents of thought are never understood, though one be well versed in classic French. Among young men generally, especially in the Latin quarter, the conversational ball scarcely rolls in any other than dialect grooves, and is nearly as puzzling to the provincial Frenchman on his first arrival as to the foreigner. In English, the epigram is cumbrous; in French, it is at home in the club, the salon, and the street.

A timid young man sits in a railway carriage opposite to a French Fotheringay, whom he hugely admires but dare not address. He softly approaches his foot until — unspeakable joy! — it touches hers. This elicits from her:

"Dites-moi que vous m'aimez, jeune homme, s'il le faut; mais pour l'amour du ciel ne me crottez pas les bottes."

Who other than a French actress could say this? A gamin opens a cab door to let a man out before a theatre, who asks him if the piece has begun yet.

"Pas encore, mon ambassadeur; on vous attend."

In this there is *blague* and epigram.

These examples are dipped up from the popular stream, where the water is somewhat muddy. Higher up at the sources, epigrammatic humor is furnished of crystal purity by such masters as Gustave Droz, Edmond About, and Alexandre Dumas the younger. These three, perhaps, bear the palm in delicacy and incisiveness.

The power of phrase in daily life is remarkable. A journalistic charge of clever words, that hits the bull's-eye of public favor, brings celebrity in twenty-four hours. The "*et ta soeur?*" uttered in the *Famille Benoiton* of Sardou, speedily runs through France to its extremities. The grandiloquent word clusters of Victor Hugo, in spite of their ludicrous side, hold a secure place in the national heart. A Frenchman may resist to the death, and, when all other means of subduing fail, a phrase disarms him. Epigram and woman are the two mistresses who share his heart, and they are nowhere wooed with such assiduity as on French soil. The popular newspapers, such as the "Gaulois" and "Figaro," are not devoted to news or leaders, but used as anvils to beat out those little showers of epigrammatic sparks which so charm the Parisians; and the men of the pen are all well supported by those of the pencil, in a style of art in delineation to which as yet we are unaccustomed.

CHAPTER 2

Gallantry

HIS EMBLEMATIC BIRD, the Gallic cock, typifies the Gaul, — given to showing off his fine feathers, of assiduous gallantry to the hens, possessed of strong affection for his own dunghill, always on parade.

His scarlet wattles answer to the red ribbon of the Legion of Honor, and the crest feathers to the Grand Cross. Cut off the rainbow feathers which he wears around his neck, the glorious wattles, the proud sweeping tail, and the cock is unhappy. Misfortune takes the name of rain, and he gives up under it completely, belittles himself, and drags his tail on the ground, as if he were on the way to the spit to be offered up on the sacrificial table of man. Let the sun come out from the rain-exhausted clouds, he brightens up directly, dries himself with despatch, and resumes his gallant, crowing life, as if such a thing as rain never existed. There is only one delightful spot in the world, and that is his own farmyard; all other farmyards and dunghills are sorry affairs; his is the home of the fat worm and fine grain; his hens are gayer, prettier, — in short, possess a *chic* given to no other hens; here, in a word, is paradise. The dove competes with him on the field of delicate attentions to the other sex, — but quietly, unobtrusively, and sentimentally: the cock is ostentatious, making his court with much cock-a-doodle-doo and wing-scraping, and a spice of humbuggery, for he often calls the hen for the grain of corn which he gobbles up himself. In matters of the heart and spur there is no middle course with him; there must be either brilliant victory or utter discomfiture. Conveyed away from his

Eden barnyard, the chivalric bird droops with nostalgia, and degenerates in race.

Whatever the Frenchman's notion may be of the *galant homme,* his ambition is always to be considered *un homme galant.* Scarcely any misfortune or inferiority of looks can rob him of the impression that he possesses certain qualities pleasing to the gentle sex. If his back be curved, he will find in it the line of beauty; if his nose be twisted, he will discover in it a piquant departure from the ordinary monotonous rule of facial feature. He fights hard against Nature where she attempts to take away from him the role he covets by playing some freak with his face or his body. If she makes him too fat, he tightly laces his unwieldy girth, and moves with a lightsome agility, to remove the impression of unusual stoutness. If she takes away the hair from the top of his head, he employs extraordinary ingenuity in bringing up the forlorn-hope of hairs from the sides to hide the loss of their brethren on the top, vanquished by Time.

His chief adversary in wooing the reputation of a gallant man is age, which ungratefully turns upon him in the decline of life, and takes away his arms; yet he persistently ignores their loss to the last. The French Major Pendennis, agreeably adorned, neglects scarcely any occasion to show himself to that sex whose lifelong slave he has been. That day does not count in his existence where he may not spend an hour or two on the Boulevard, in admiring the houris* of his earthly paradise, as they pass before him in equipage and afoot, in a never-ending procession. That night is a meagre one where he may not stand in an orchestra stall at the *Italiens,* with his back to the stage, to gaze on those princesses to whom he has sworn eternal fealty, or to promenade in the *foyer,* and perchance whisper in two or three of their ears a brace or two of his handsomely-turned compliments.

In the hands of the Gaul, gallantry is elaborated into an art.

---

* Women of voluptuous, almost perfect beauty.

Nature does more for him than for the inhabitant of any other country in this way, and by culture he crowns the edifice. It is as difficult, he says, to be a gallant man as to be a poet; there must be the existing faculty as a foundation, then comes the superstructure of education. To be gallant, from his point of view, is to be possessed of tact, refinement, intelligence, taste, and an adoration for women, young and old, beautiful and ugly. The rules of the art cannot be written (according to French authority); but they are divined by inspiration of its votaries. No rule, for instance, is necessary to teach one of them to take off his hat to a woman whom he meets on the stairway; he knows that, as he knows how to eat or sleep.

The finesse and strategy which the woman as passive employs to him as active is remarkable. An expression of the eye, a movement of the lips, a posture of the body, a gesture of the hand, convey to him words which he reads running. In the woman of the salon, there is a tacit invitation to the man to be aggressive, — to make her *une petite cour inoffensive,* which he on all occasions considers to be a duty. This sort of an invitation may be so vague as to be almost imperceptible, yet it is there, concealed behind a labyrinth of manner. As a rule, she does this without any idea of transgressing generally accepted rules of morality. It is the desire to exercise the especial powers of her sex for an hour or two, as an agreeable variety to the home duties of the woman of family; but it sometimes proves to be a dangerous pastime. It is her nature to please wherever she finds herself, in public or in private. In the absence of her own species, she fondles the cat or canary bird; with her husband she is full of those *agaceries* and *douceurs,* which contribute the chief joy to his domestic life. As long as there is a man in her presence, he assumes an integral importance denied to those of her sex, and is more her natural complement, apparently, than in countries where women are satisfied to pass so much of their time with each other.

She is the acknowledged deity of her drawing-room; and each gallant man who enters, hat in hand, — a custom which disposes of the question of what is a man to do with his hands, the object to which he clings being called the *planche de salut,* — knows, from certain indications veiled from the vulgar, the impression which he produces on his hostess. Nothing is more natural than her *pose* as she sits in her drawing-room, because it is the perfection, of art. The soft light which falls over her, the color of the background against which she sits, the stray tendril of hair escaping from the rest, the kind of expression which plays about her face, the carefully modulated tones of her voice, never rising to harshness or a high key, the subservient and auxiliary hues of her apparel, the graceful manoeuvring of her hands — all these are made the subject of close study, and consummate art is made to look like simple nature. The ordinary affairs of life are invested with this general grace: she listens to a tedious recital with apparently as much interest as to an enlivening one, for want of politeness is heresy: the simple act of passing a cup of tea is accompanied with a look and gesture which are irresistible. The knowledge and performance of this dilettanteism of daily life are sometimes even made a test of general capacity, as was done by the Marquise de Créquy in the case of Franklin. Although the philosopher was popular with the French people generally, as the representative of democracy, he was disliked by the leading aristocrats, like Louis XVI, Marie Antoinette, and Madame de Créquy. The latter thought him anything but gallant. At a repast where she sat alongside of him, and where he was habited in the memorable brown coat, brown waistcoat, breeches of same, and cravat striped with red, she thus records her impression: "That which I saw most remarkable in him was his mode of eating eggs. He emptied five or six into a goblet, mingling salt, pepper, and butter, and thus made a *joli ragoût philadelphique.* He cut with his knife the pieces of melon he wished to eat; and he bit the asparagus, in place of cutting off the point with his knife on the plate, and eating it properly with a fork. You perceive it was the mode of a savage."

Thus, in the estimation of the marquise, the doctor's discoveries in electricity, his practical benevolence and wisdom, his work in the cause of freedom and civilization, were held of little account before the fact that he did not conduct himself at table like the courtiers of her time. She would not deign to talk with him on this occasion; and his genial soul, she gives us to understand, was frozen into silence by her hauteur. If there was want of affability on the part of Franklin in this instance, there is fearful record to the contrary in a note which he wrote to Madame Helvétius, in which he endeavors to compete with Frenchmen on their own ground; and the fact of his having done so in a language of which he betrays ludicrously imperfect knowledge, leaves one to infer, considering his ordinary prudence, that the charms of Madame Helvétius were of a most incendiary character.

In bestowing a favor in France, there is always an eye to the surroundings. The cross of the Legion of honor, with the insignia and patent, is sent by the late emperor in an Easter egg to one of his favorite ministers. The Duchess of Gerolstein is the recipient of a brougham enclosed in a monster egg of wood. An Arab sheik performs the Oriental *fantasia* on horseback before Louis Napoleon: in the heat and excitement of the performance, he throws off his jacket, and when he picks it up afterward he finds the red ribbon attached to the button-hole.

In comparison with the rude covering with which the Briton clothes his acts, the pliant grace and kindly solicitude of the Gaul in presence of his fellow-men compel admiration. Yet, if one could read the heart of this Briton, it would, perhaps, be found that his sentiments of humanity are deeper than those of his neighbor. The rudest husk sometimes covers the sweetest kernel. When the Gaul performs a gallant act, he extracts all the honey that is to be gotten out of it. If he gives up his seat to a woman, he takes off his hat, and points to the vacant place as if he were surrendering an empire, and inviting a queen to enthrone herself thereon. If he hoists her umbrella, it is as if he were spreading out the canopy of heaven over her head. If he picks up a fallen glove, he offers it to the owner as if he were placing his sword and honor at her disposal for the rest of his life. If he quits her at the foot of a stairway, he looks after her as a chamberlain of the court might do when her Majesty mounts the throne. And in each instance the woman meets him half way in grace and affability. All this makes him happy. The consciousness of having conducted himself as a chevalier without reproach, the probability of having produced an impression on the heart of her whom he has thus encountered, and the recollection of her enticing manner, bring ripples of pleasure across his mind whenever the scene recurs to him.

The Frenchman's politeness is carried to great lengths. He bows with a coup de chapeau, in the Bois, to the Laïs of the Lake, or in the public gardens. He holds conversation with her at the theatre, in sight of those who are entitled to receive his legitimate homage. He bestows costly favors on her which should be conferred elsewhere. Many an Anglo-Saxon would do the same were he unseen; and this is one of the most striking differences between the two men: one does certain acts of which he is ashamed, and which he covers with a cloak of seeming virtue; the other, as a rule, makes no attempt to hide these things and assume the air of one who holds them in aversion. Morally, there is perhaps but little difference between them; yet the Englishman is always endeavoring to appear the better man under his mask of prim conventionality, which irritates the other, who charges him with being a Tartuffe, — in short, a hypocrite.

There is an elasticity and adaptability in the Gaul, in presence of the woman, of which the Anglo-Saxon has but a meagre share.

The former, before all classes of the sex, cat-like, falls on his feet, be she countess, bourgeoise, or grisette; and to be brought unexpectedly in contact with any of them never seems to disconcert or even surprise him. The Anglo-Saxon is taken at a disadvantage under similar circumstances, from which he does not rally immediately. The susceptibility of the newly-arrived foreigner, for example, is put to a rude trial when he buys a pair of gloves. Behind the counter stand several smiling, self-possessed young women, whose eyes turn on him with disconcerting steadiness. He approaches the nearest of them, and signifies his desire to make a purchase. Are the gloves for monsieur? They are. Will monsieur give himself the trouble to sit down before the counter? He slips on to a high stool which brings his head on a level with hers. She purringly inquires his number, which he generally does not know, when she daintily measures the masculine hand, holding it, after the tape measurement, lightly by the finger tips, to examine the form of the glove required. She in the same tone inquires his color, to which a Gaul would probably reply, "Whatever your taste may suggest;" but to which the newly-arrived foreigner gives an answer destitute of any kind of embroidery. When she softly takes his hand in hers again, and looks into his face with a smile, Americus begins to think that this is indeed a tender business. Before, however, he has time to make many reflections on the situation, she is at work on the hand, and slips on the glove, caressingly introduces the fingers, the operation sandwiched with arch glances and chirrupy speech, and then the glove is buttoned, and the last fold smoothed out with a gentle pat. This incendiary performance is followed with the question whether monsieur will have his other hand treated in the same way. The moth, of course, will have another go at the candle; and, by the time he is through, he is naturally somewhat singed. Happily for family peace, the betrothed Mary Jane or the espoused Mary Ann cannot look into his heart at that moment. The eyes of the feminine Mephistopheles behind the counter follow out his retiring figure with a slight elevation of the eyebrows, and a terrible monosyllable uttered to one of her companions.

The modest foreigner goes through another ordeal with the flower-girl. With a smile as bright and attractive as her flowers, she asks him if he will not have one. He would prefer not to encounter those winning eyes, and endeavors to pass on, but he may not do so: she holds him as securely as the Ancient Mariner held the wedding guest, and he signifies his acceptance of the tendered opening bud. He may not receive it with his hands: she with her nimble fingers will attach it to his button-hole, and the embarrassed man stands while the girl fondles over the region of his heart, and looks into the whites of his half-averted eyes. And the havoc thus committed in ten short minutes may not be repaired in six months. There is no fixed price for such a favor; and he is told, with an expression that would have troubled the soul of St. Anthony, that it is anything he may please to give. His betrothed Belinda, alas! would think it dear at any price.

In doubling the capes of critical situations in adroit, evasive phrase, no one is equal to the Frenchman. This faculty pervades all classes, and is seen in the daily life and correspondence of high and low. When Madame de Staël asks Talleyrand whom he would save first from drowning, were she and a certain other woman—her rival—in the water at the same time, the diplomatist replies that he cannot swim. A woman declines to be godmother to an expected child, as she will be absent when the interesting event transpires; but appreciates the honor, and deeply regrets that she cannot avail herself of it. This is known to be a refusal; but is clothed in such a form that no exception can be made to it, and pleasant relations are conserved. A father refuses the hand of his daughter to a young man, saying that he feels flattered by the proposition; and if his daughter were not too young, or had more experience of life, or something else, nothing would give him greater pleasure than to become his father-in-law. Here again is refusal smoothed with a graceful covering. Even a woman-servant, in declining an offer of marriage, knows how to say that she is persuaded it would be very difficult to find a better husband than he who proposes; but for reasons which have nothing to do with him, and which she cannot explain, she is obliged to decline, although she thanks him all the same. A sick man is never told that he looks badly, should he be at death's door. A plain woman is made to forget her want of good looks by an adroit reference to some supposed compensating quality. Everybody is handsome, well dressed, happy, and the picture of health; the round of life — "O que c'est comme un bouquet de fleurs," as says the popular refrain in the "Little Ebonist."

But stern moralists say this is equivocation and lying, and it is true; but the equivocation yields harmony, and the lies are as white as lilies. Through them the rude asperities along life's journey are softened or made to disappear. Graceful evasions and snow-white lies go about like sisters of charity, in this case, to heal and soothe, but not to wound. They are faults, but faults whose extenuations transform them almost into virtues.

Occupations do not absorb Frenchmen to an extent to render them averse to social commerce; and, however well they may work, they set apart a certain portion of time to the amenities of life. From the seriousness required in work to the good humor exhibited in play, the transition is rapid; and the harness is resumed as quickly as it is thrown off. With Anglo-Saxons, as a rule, the pursuit of any higher kind of vocation renders them unfit to be men of the world: they get wound up so tightly in their affairs that they cannot be unstrung, and are so trammelled by the artificial forms of society that they are prone to renounce it altogether as interfering with the serious aims of life. Thus the life of the Anglo-Saxon seems to be special, while that of the Gaul is dual. In the latter, ambition in science or art is generally accompanied by the necessity of social expansion, and the two thus march together in harmony. In the gatherings of the polite world, where people meet on common ground, there is a levelling process, which often brings the ordinary man up to the man of genius; for the former at times throws off sudden impressions and fancies with a facility and grace denied to the latter. Nicolle, the great moralist, speaking of this scintillant elegant of the salon, said, "He conquers me in the drawing-room, but he surrenders to me at discretion on the staircase."

The Gaul is seldom so absorbed in any occupation as to lose his taste for society. He has a natural tendency in this direction, which is developed by education. He is a musician who sings and plays passably well, and is an excellent critic. He draws, and perhaps paints more or less, which furnishes him with sufficient knowledge to be a conscientious amateur in painting and sculpture. He has a natural taste for poetry, and can write tolerable verses with a certain ease. He is given to fencing and waltzing, and exhibits taste in his dress and surroundings. Every contribution is employed, that science and art have to offer, that will add to the charm of social life. Conversation is practised as an art, where epigram, grace, and vivacity are constantly exhibited. Habitual speech is flowery and flattering. Thus his character is fuller than that of the specialist across the Channel, whose accomplishments are usually confined to such things as British politics, horse pleasures, a dead language or two, and shooting half-tame pheasants.

Amid the rudest trials to which man is subjected, the Gaul will not neglect what he considers the niceties of his person, — his capers and grimaces. In the hurry of a busy day he will find time to make an ode to his mistress's eyebrow, or to send her a bouquet. On his wedding day, his buoyant spirits will not destroy his grace of language, and in his last words at the hour of death he will still observe the proprieties of art. The pleasures of society are wooed with ardor when young, and not abandoned in old age. Voltaire, at a very advanced age, endeavors to dance with a lady, saying as he does so, "On dit que c'est le premier pas qui coûte, moi, je trouve que c'est le dernier." And I have myself observed an aged ambassador of France, in private theatricals, who entered on the functions of *souffleur* with the ardor of a young man of twenty.

The wide dissemination of art-feeling has a refining tendency on the manners of all classes. Beautiful squares and parks, with walks and shady forests, fountains and lakes, are open to all. The eyes of the people are made familiar with architectural beauty as exhibited in the boulevards, bridges, and public edifices of the great city. The magnificent art-galleries are free to all who wish to see them, and the working people visit them frequently, especially on Sundays and *fête* days, when they are kept open for their benefit. The round of Pierre's and Justine's recreation on these holidays usually begins with a visit to the Louvre, the Luxembourg, or the Exposition, before they are off on sylvan junketings; and this habit of being brought face to face with art has an influence on their lives. Thus the man in blouse is often familiar with the great pictures of French masters. In the houses of the poor, there are no vapid, keepsake heads in glowing colors, but copies of pictures exhibiting more or less merit. The deep red and blue Daniel in the Lion's Den, and the doll-faced Mary Ann, surrounded with an inch of bright mahogany, are not seen on their walls. The square, loud-striking, and loud-ticking clock in red wood, and the plaster-of-paris rabbit or cat painted in unnatural hues, have no places on their mantles. In humble cafés are found pictures which would be considered fit to hang in some of the best restaurants of London and New York. The signs over shops show a talent not possessed by our sign-painters, and many a *gargote* has grapes and vine-leaves painted over its door which merit a better place.

To see the orderly, smiling people dressed in their best, going through the galleries of a Sunday, or sauntering in the parks to enjoy nature and hear the music, is not an unpleasant sight; and it is difficult to believe, for this, that they are on the road to perdition. It is doubtful if the same classes across the Channel occupy themselves as well on the day of rest.

One of the indications of the general spread of art is, that it is found even in the worst classes. The criminal hero of fiction among rogues in London is the brutal Blueskin, without any extenuating wit or manner; in Paris it is Robert Macaire, who, it is true, stops at nothing in swindling and robbery, but attaches much importance to the form. Blueskin kills with an oath; Macaire sends his victim into the next world, politely apologizing for the necessity of the act. When Monsieur Macaire takes the property of another, he borrows it with polite speech and profound bow. His conversation is full of high-flown sentiment, accompanied with majestic attitudes. The artistic get-up of this dandy rogue of rents and patches, with his creaking snuff-box and club-stick, his bland imperturbability and unscrupulous philosophy, his dilapidated hat gayly cocked on one side, is so impressed on the mind, that one is almost constrained to believe that the man really existed. To kindred souls in the Faubourg Saint Antoine there never was such a taking rogue as this; and better people were never tired of his dandified airs and rags, as represented on the stage by Frédéric Lemaître, or portrayed by the pencils of clever artists like Philipon and Daumier, one of whose happiest efforts was where Monsieur Macaire, arrayed in kingly garments, gives royal opinions of a pernicious character to his follower Bertrand, who receives them with the commentary of, "Ah, vieux blagueur, va." The Faubourg St. Antoine laughed over these oddities until the tears ran down its cheeks; but it would have turned away from the brutalities of Blueskin with disgust.

There is an uncontrollable desire to cajole or caress whatever is liked, be it man, woman, child, or animal. Those who do not fancy this affectionate familiarity must employ stern dignity as a fender. They have a proverb to the effect that they will end by eating out of the hand of even the most illustrious person, if encouraged. They soon familiarize themselves with the most awe-inspiring creature, which in the end may increase their affection, but lessens their admiration. The god-like is short-lived. Their affectionate nature must find expression somewhere. In the absence of children, it breaks out upon lapdogs, thoroughbred terriers, cats, and birds. The solicitude of a childless couple is employed concerning the health of Tabby or Towser, and it is a common spectacle to see the woman leading the gayly caparisoned little terrier up the Elysian Fields for the benefit of his digestion, stopping occasionally to allow the creature to get his wind and repose his little tan-colored legs. It is a case of killing with kindness; for the animal often becomes plethoric, wheezy, and dyspeptic from over care and feeding. And what a wealth of sweetness is bestowed on this spoiled pet! It is, "Come here, Bibi, and let me nurse you;" "Will Bibi have a piece of sugar?" "Who loves Bibi most?" "Does Bibi love the little mistress?" "She adores Bibi, va!"—this, accompanied with cajoling caress. A satirist avers that the woman often does this in the presence of a man to make him wish he were a dog; and, although one cannot credit her with such intent, the result is often attained.

The woman coquets with the canary-bird in the same fashion, in the absence of other society. She enters upon tender and animated conversations with it, which sound like a page or two of "Romeo and Juliet," where she plays double, putting the questions, and making the answers; and, if the bird have any heart, one would think he must be captivated by such *roucoulement* beyond release. The purring cat, which is here so often likened to her own sex, also comes in for his share of the mistress's tender assiduities, and lolls about in the favor of her smiles.

The extravagance of French politeness has been remarkable in the past. Three centuries ago there was such an ado when two people met, that the Chevalier Marin said that all conversation began with a ballet. Fourscore years ago, graceful antics and high-flown compliments were still in vogue; but the deep triplicate salutation, with the "Beautiful marquise, your bewitching eyes make me die of love," passed away with the revolution of '93. The eccentricities of gallant speech and gallant acts constitute one of the principal arteries running through the body politic, from its earliest history to the present time. Under cover of the French dictum that it is impossible to be too polite, singular extremes are reached, especially by the elderly men who affect something of the Regency manners. In some cases it is carried to a point where it might be called the gymnastics of social intercourse, — where the man insists on keeping his bald head uncovered in a hot sun, or runs with hot haste to convey a lapdog to a woman waiting, or bows low with a grand swoop of the hat to another man whom he sees two or three times a day. There is an historical instance of a well-known, aged nobleman, who, descending the stairway, meets a youth of twenty mounting; the nobleman stops to let him go up, and the youth does the same, inviting the former to pass down; the nobleman stands firm, and requests the youth to continue, who responds, "Jamais!" with hand on heart; he knows too well what youth owes to age: upon which the elder *commands* him to mount; when the young man, with a bow, says, "Youth owes obedience to age," and passes, thus saving the situation, as he believes.

The Anglo-Saxon does not often give way to such eccentricities of sentiment. His colder temperament and extreme conscientiousness hold the heart's tongue in check, and unpremeditated acts of gallantry are not frequent in the race. Walter Raleigh throwing his mantle on the ground for the royal feet to pass over, and the king picking up the leg-bracelet of the Countess of Salisbury, accompanied with the "Honi soit que mal y pense," are rare instances, and borrowed at that from Norman chivalry.

The love of the Anglo-Saxon may be deeper, but its expression is more passionate in the Gaul. In one it may be a smouldering volcano: in the other it is fiery lava bursting forth. The outpouring of the heart runs through the Frenchman's daily life, his literature, and his music. In his love-stories the plot moves on with *crescendo* action. When Gounod's love-smitten Faust, in the garden-scene, throws himself at the feet of Marguerite, and carols his "Laisse moi contempler ton visage," sympathy throbs in the breast of the Gaul; but when, a few minutes later, Marguerite, in her supreme, sublimated happiness, — a sort of adieu to earth and earthly things, — holds her lover in her arms, and cries, "Pour toi je veux mourir," an electric shock is communicated to this spectator, and he shouts "Bravo," with tears in his eyes.

Thus the Gaul is full of action before his adored, she meeting him part of the way; and he hurries into the country of the Tender, and threads its labyrinths with glowing ardor. The Anglo-Saxon cannot throw himself into the business with this abandon: he is haunted by an apprehension of doing something foolishly sentimental, and he clings to his cold reserve. The Gaul burns his vessels, and talks of death or possession, a cottage by the lake, two hearts as one, and the rest of it. And this mercurial lover assuredly believes every word that he utters — at the time. He affirms that we are cold and hard; in a word, that we are not affectionate like him. When it is urged that we feel as much as he under our mask of impassibility, he shrugs, which is his most common sign of incredulity. Supposing this to be the case, for the sake of argument, he will say, "What is the use of a flower that none can smell or see?" The question *is* pertinent, and furnishes food for reflection.

When he falls in love, he plunges into the ears, — for in this he is a man of no half-way measures, — and commits what we consider acts of folly. He attacks with impetuosity, and avers that we cold, slow-moving people do not understand love-making; that, whilst we are skirmishing at the gate, he would be in the citadel. He is full of it to running over, and, if the course of love moves on smoothly, he goes about among his friends, and tells them what an angel she is, and how happy he is; he takes out of the pocket covering his heart, her portrait, slipper, or what not, and, religiously kissing the treasure, shows it to sympathetic eyes. He is capable of getting into her coupe, and sitting down in her vacated seat, and of finding enjoyment in the act; of taking out of the omnium gatherum of the vehicle, with a feverish curiosity, the little ivory mirror in which it is her wont to scan her lovely features and arrange a straying tress, the last novel marked at the place where her beautiful eyes last dwelt, the paper-cutter which her sweet hand held to cut the leaves; and of bestowing the honors of osculation on each of these objects. He does not rest satisfied until he has pointed her out to one or more intimate friends at the church or the theatre, accompanied with the inevitable question, "Eh bien, comment la trouve-tu, mon cher?" Whereupon these polite friends strike the key-note of the lover's idyl, and affirm with enthusiasm that she is an angel.

In their gallantry, the French are often comedians without knowing it. To tell where genuine feeling ends and counterfeit begins, would be difficult. It is not assumed with any sinister design, but is an inoffensive desire, in the absence of the real, to play with the semblance. It is grown children's "make-believe," is called posing and is a national trait. There are all kinds of posing; but the most common is that which is brought into play between the sexes, where man assumes those airs calculated to disturb woman's peace of mind, and where she resembles an angel condescending to visit this poor earth to dally a few moments with this adorer. The comedy between them is not without interest. When they become acquainted, there is flow of gallant speech and adroit response. To them silence is not gold, but time is; and they hasten to the bower of Cupid. Jules swears, that, if she will not accept him, he will throw himself into the Seine: she may not believe a word of this, but oh, how sweet to hear! He loves her to distraction; none other ever loved as he loves; and the worn platitude is as fresh and sweet as new-made chocolate-drops to the listening Léontine. How much of this is true, and how much is false? Alas! Jules does not know himself.

Of these comedians, the student-rower of the Latin Quarter is one of the most conspicuous. His preparations would lead one to suppose that he was going to do the work of one of the Oxford or Cambridge crew. He arrays himself in white flannel shirt with pink border, and trousers the same; a nautical necktie issues from a great turn-down collar, and a gayly-bordered cap is set jauntily on one side of his head. Thus accoutred, he starts for Marny with Fifine, on whom his costume produces its intended effect. At his destination, by appointment, he meets two or three other *canotiers* with their respective Fifines, when they form a some-what noisy group, and the *tutoiement* is the general order of speech. They repeat the smart words and puns they have heard in the theatre or on the street, accompanied with gestures some-what extravagant. They paddle about in the water an hour, smoke a number of pipes, and laugh at the sallies of their Fifines, who are so droll. When the *canotier* returns to the town, and goes to his café in the evening, he tells those whom he meets that he has been rowing until he is *éreinté*. The pull was terrible; but he is so inured to this kind of thing, he doesn't mind it.

To lie on his back under a shady tree, with a pipe in his mouth and an arm around Fifine's waist, is probably a more agreeable way of passing the time than pulling stroke in a boat; but Adolphe is not satisfied with this bucolic picture, and must needs spin his yarn. Fifine's opinion of this kind of boating is, that it is simply delightful. She shares with him the pleasures of the café as well as the rowing, and takes her beer, and joins in the general convivality. She is something loud in voice and laughter, and said to be more naughty than the canotier's Fifine of a score of years ago. But Fifine in her pouting moments has something to say for herself, and avers that Adolphe of today is degenerate; then falls upon the whole sex, exclaiming, "Oh, les hommes, les hommes! Quelle canaille!" This, however, is only a fleeting cloud which passes between them, and in ten minutes it disappears altogether. Then she cajoles him again, and calls him "mon petit chat" and "mon petit monstre," peace is effectually restored, and additional books are ordered to cement it.

The café-restaurant usually frequented by Adolphe and his Fifine is kept by someone from the province of the former, who gives him credit, being acquainted with the circumstances of his family. Here Adolphe orders generously for self and Fifine, and never troubles himself about verifying accounts. Fifine thinks it is like fairyland: you order a dinner, it appears, and no questions asked. This goes on until Adolphe, now a lawyer, is settled down in his provincial home, when the proprietor of the restaurant gives him a shock as from a galvanic battery, in the way of a well-charged bill. If he is not in a position to pay, the shock is communicated to his father, who unties the purse-strings with many shakings of the head and Mon Dieus, — ah, the young men were not like that in *his* day! Or, he makes a marriage of convenience, and gets the required amount out of his wife's dowry. Here are the dregs of the flowing bowl which was drunk with so much Don Giovanni laissez-aller, in the society of the too amiable Fifine.

In this way does Cupid find the way to Fifine's heart: As she hurries up the Boulevard Saint Michel, or passes through the Luxembourg Garden, caught in the rain, a student of the Quarter — an Adolphe — steps forward, and offers his umbrella with himself, to shield her from the elements: she probably at first declines, but the chivalric young man politely insists on her not exposing herself to the shower; she wavers, when he hoists the umbrella, and walks away with her without further parley; and this he calls the *coup de parapluie*. It is the beginning of his acquaintance with Fifine, and in three weeks they look as if they had known each other for three years. He goes to her shop at closing time, and conducts her to her home in the bird-like nest at the top of the house. On Sundays and fête-days he lounges with her in the Luxembourg Garden; or the twain get into a third-class railway carriage, and go to Montmorency to eat cherries, or to Enghien to sail on the lake, or, better still, to Robinson to ride the donkeys, and finish up the day in dining in the branches of the colossal restaurant-tree, so popular with the grisette and the young man of the Latin Quarter.

Thus the day is what we must regard as a reprehensible round of gayety. Adolphe says life is short, and Fifine repeats it; then they sing in chorus, "Let us be merry while we may, for tomorrow we die." Or perhaps Adolphe first encounters the bright eyes of Fifine as she stands behind the counter of a magasin, in which case the course of his love does not run so swiftly as if he made the *coup de parapluie*. If it be a chocolate shop which contains Fifine, here will he buy of the toothsome stuff two or three times a day in order to exchange sweets for sweets, his compliments being more sacchariferous than his purchases. But she only laughs at these sweet words, for she has often heard them before, — "Les hommes, voyez-vous, ce sont des farceurs."

In spite of these discouraging words, for she loves to be dearly won, Adolphe at length finds favor in her sight. Then does he hang in her ears rings of pure gold, and crown her pretty head with a new hat. Then be in the bucolic excursions to Bougival, the dinners in summer-houses on the borders of lakes and streams, the dancing, the riding of wooden horses at neighboring fairs, and swinging in circular swings, the consultation of fortune-tellers, the saunterings in the woods, the conjugation of the verb to love, in which the "M'aime-tu" and "Je t'aime" are especially and eternally dwelt upon.

The purse of Adolphe is a meagre one at best, and, after two or three weeks of this junketing, becomes transparently thin. The pleasures of his idol and himself may be dispensed with, but the necessities of life must be paid for until the remittance arrives from home. This he calls being *à sec;* and when in this condition everything he possesses except what he has on his back passes into the hands of what he calls his aunt, and we term uncle. If this is not sufficient to bridge the impecunious days, recourse is had to the earrings and silk robe of Fifine, which find their way to the same receptacle. These are Lenten days for the loving twain. Their diet is chastening, and the variety of their pleasures is restricted. For the time, the days of orchestra stalls, bisque, Saint Estèphe, and coffee on the Boulevards, are over. Clothed in the simple garments that are left out of the hands of the aunt, they repair to one of the Duval establishments or *a crémerie,* and make their dinner of a three-cent bouillon, boiled beef, and a piece of Brie cheese, flanked with the most ordinary of the ordinary wine. But they eat this with Saint Anthony's sauce, which makes all food palatable, — hunger, — and still laugh and amuse themselves, and find that it is not such a bad world after all. When the remittance comes, Adolphe is what he calls *à flot:* their joint wardrobe is withdrawn from the aunt, and the junketing is resumed.

At last the law is finished, and a letter comes from the father of Adolphe desiring his son to return immediately to the paternal roof in some country town or village. Then is there wailing in the abode of Fifine au sixième. Adolphe swears that he will never leave her, and the parental letter is disobeyed. Papa's second letter is pathetic: it asks the son if he wishes to bring the gray-haired locks with sorrow to the grave. Adolphe remains firm; but the woman comes to the rescue, for the parental epistle touches her heart. She loves Adolphe more than she loves herself, and counsels him to return to his home. The man is at length persuaded; and he leaves her, taking away with him her heart and the best years of her life. Adolphe goes away, saying that none other shall ever occupy his heart but the grisette, and soon marries a girl with a dowry, not half as pretty as Fifine, whom his father has long since selected for him. The rollicking student is transformed into the staid country lawyer, who is severe on the follies of youth. After his departure, the weeping in the eyry au sixième is passionate, but not of long duration. In a month or two Jacques steps forward with another umbrella to make the *coup de parapluie,* or becomes one of the best clients of the chocolate shop, and serves over the counter a rehash of Adolphe's compliments. She will hardly listen to his nonsense; for "Les hommes, voyez-vous, ce sont des farceurs; je n'en veux pas." But his nonsense is so droll she cannot help laughing, and here Jacques makes a tremendous stride; for, according to the proverbial wisdom of the great city, when the woman laughs she is half conquered. Before long Jacques is standing in the shoes of Adolphe, and new earrings and jaunty hat are the marks of victory. The junketings to Asnières and Bougival, the dinners by the borders of lakes, and the conjugation of the verb *aimer,* recommence. And during a moment of tender expansion, as they saunter in the wood of Vincennes, she confides to Jacques that she never loved Adolphe as she loves him. There were certain blemishes which marred the splendor of Adolphe, but Jacques is all refulgent with perfection. Ah, the only true love is the last! Let us be happy today, says Jacques, for tomorrow we die; Fifine repeats it with exaltation; and they whirl away in the mazes of the Closerie de Lilas to the sound of a crashing music that drowns the click of glasses and the buzz of busy tongues.

Happy Jacques! Happy Fifine!

CHAPTER 3

French Living

THE AMERICAN CRITIC says the Gaul thinks and talks too much of his dinner; and, were eating and drinking for appeasing hunger and thirst only, there would be justice in the criticism. But dinner is more than this with him. It is a symposium where psychological and sensuous pleasures are combined, — a pretext for a reunion of friends where there is as much talking as eating. This is in compliance with the Gaul's general rule of making Nature, in the exercise of her functions, yield all the pleasure of which she is capable. In his artistic hands the tearing and swallowing of his ancestors has been transformed into the sumptuous banquet adorned with flowers and beautiful women, and surrounded by mirrors, statues, and pictures. In doing this he has taken the rough diamond, and polished it to the highest degree of which it is susceptible. According to the Gallic aphorism, "Animals feed, man eats: the man of intellect alone knows *how* to eat."

A couple of diners, who belong to that brotherhood of which Brillat-Savarin was the high priest, enter the Café Anglais. They are past the prime of life, as are the greater part of the clients of this celebrated restaurant, — which, according to these elders, is a compliment to the establishment, for they aver that the young have uncultivated palates, and hence limited knowledge of food and drink. The two elderly diners saunter in, and leisurely take their seats. They have been preparing themselves since breakfast for the repast of the day in gentle out-of-door exercise; for nothing annoys them so much as not to be hungry at the appointed hour. They select their snow-white table near one of the windows looking on the boulevard, in order that the sight may be pleased with the passing promenaders at the same time that the taste is gratified with nourishment. They settle themselves comfortably in their easy leather chairs, as a soft-voiced waiter presents them with the bill of fare without asking what they want, well knowing that they require time for reflection. In an ordinary restaurant he fires off his "Monsieur désire?" like a shot; but here he gracefully retires to leave them to that meditation which the importance of the subject demands. Their sight is not so good as their palates, and they have recourse to the *monocle,* or eye-glasses, to scan, as a Mohammedan does the Koran, the choice bit of literature which the waiter has left with them, and taste of the happiness of anticipation. To the gourmets this is the preliminary pleasure of the dinner, and is counted on as one of its features. Having carefully read through the bill of fare, from pottage to dessert, there is discussion as to selection; but discussion of an easy kind, that rather sharpens than dulls the fine edge of appetite. Were they seated in the Foreign Affairs Department on the other side of the Seine, they might be taken for diplomats discussing each separate provision of an international treaty.

At length the selections are made: for example, a simple soup, a carp à la Chambord, a capon stuffed with Périgord truffles, a pheasant à la Sainte Alliance, tenderest of asparagus with sauce à l'omazôme, a dish of ortolans à la Provençale, a pyramid of méringues à la vanille, and finally a bit of Brie cheese; for the great Savarin has laid it down that a dinner without cheese is like a pretty woman with only one eye. And the swift but smoothly-gliding waiter takes the prandial programme to the horn of plenty in the rear, which pours out its treasures year in and year out before the most critical clients of Europe. The wine is more quickly chosen, for these sybarites know the cellar by heart, — that famous cellar which runs midway under the street. One course after another is taken leisurely, and the pleasure of the occupation long drawn out. They say, "We are not pressed; let us eat at our leisure, for we always have the time to die." They are of the highest guild in gastronomy, and are able to discover the superior flavor of the leg of the partridge on which it has slept, and in what latitude a grape has ripened from the wine they sip. In eating, they experience what they call the three sensations, — the direct, the complete, and the sensation of the judgment; in drinking, in addition to these sensations, those of gutturation, and the last, — the after-taste of perfume or fragrance which for a time remains. Pleasant wit and gentle cachinnation* are courted as auxiliaries to lengthen the appetite and promote digestion. An hour and a half to two hours is devoted to the repast; and when the end is reached three bottles of their dear friends of the cellar are pleasantly at work under their waistcoats, in assisting digestion. In their gentle exhilaration they feel the need of locomotion; they saunter out on the boulevard arm in arm, and find each other and all the world delightful. They lounge to the Rue de la Paix or the Madeleine, and back to the Café Napolitain, renowned for its coffee, where they take seats at one of the outside tables on the broad asphalte, and sip fragrant coffee to a fragrant cigar. According to them, the coffee pushes the dinner, which is followed by the sacramental tiny glass of cognac, in its turn, to push the coffee. Thus the dinner marches in single-file discipline from soup to cognac, like the queue entering a popular theatre. Or it is a construction of regular layers, whose cellar is soup, the ground floor the pièce de résistance, the upper stories the lighter courses, and the crowning of the edifice coffee and cognac; the chimneys being the wines which run through them all — after leaving the cellar — to warm and brighten.

The happy twain, according to Lavater, are born gourmets: they have round and square faces, sparkling eyes, small foreheads, short noses, full lips, and round chins. They congratulate

* Loud convulsive laughter.

themselves that they are what they are; that they are not absent-minded business men, nor ambitious men, who eat and think at the same time. The aphorisms of their high priest are often on their tongues, such as, "Tell me what you eat, and I will tell you what you are," and "The fate of nations depends on how they are fed." They belong to an extensive brotherhood. The stranger brethren may not recognize each other away from the feast; but, from the moment they sit opposite each other over a savory dish or a toothsome glass, the recognition is mutual; as soon even as the incense of a soigné potage rises to their nostrils, the ties which bind them are revealed. Then they are happy; for next to eating a good dinner is the pleasure of a comrade to eat it with, —a comrade possessing the genius of the palate, who is able to march abreast through all the delightful labyrinths of taste. A companion of the baser kind, who eats to live, is worse than none, for his presence wounds the sensitive soul of him who lives to eat.

Such is the devotion of some of the bachelor gourmets to the table, that they do not consider the presence of women desirable, alleging as an excuse that they are faulty in the taste of food and wine, that they are consumers of the saccharine and the acid, which are injurious to a good mouth. Not that these bachelors love the better half of their kind less, but the table more; and they lay it down as a rule to themselves, that, unless the women are known to be of their guild, they may not be invited to the feast. These finical epicures, however, are not embraced in the general category of gourmets, who gallantly hold out against separating the women from their table, and strive to have them together as one of the most harmonious combinations.

These are among the frequenters of the Café Anglais, where the addition runs to a figure beyond the resources of the ordinary purse. It has a vogue — especially in wine — greater than any other establishment, which must be paid for, although it may be no better than half a dozen others, such as Véry, Véfour, Philippe, Trois Frères, and Magny and Foyer on the other side of the Seine. In the Café Anglais are the reefs on which many a young man has been wrecked. With us men often ruin themselves through alcohol, profligacy, and gambling, but rarely from eating. We can understand the passion for drink and gambling, but not that for food whose indulgence turns rich men into beggars. The man who even expresses a taste for the *art de la gueule* with us is regarded with general disfavor. In France men occasionally eat themselves out of house and home. In Columbus land, among a certain class of Puritans, the love of the flesh-pots may not be manifested, and the stomach is ignored; to dwell on the attractions of écrévisses au vin de Sauterne and pain de volaille à la suprême is sinful, and the pumpkin pie and hot biscuit must be taken with silent resignation. The Gaul says, that, if they had his kitchen and his palate cultivation, they would commit the follies of which he is guilty; but this only relaxes the hard lines of their Pilgrim Rock faces into a smile of commiseration.

There are a number of what are called second class restaurants, such as Voisin, Vachette, Durand, which to a gourmet not too exacting are as good as those that have been named, and are chiefly patronized by Frenchmen who understand prices as well as eating. They are not in vogue, and this is a sufficient reason to the young man of fashion for not frequenting them. He goes, when out of his club-house, to one of the English taverns, of which there are several of an inferior kind in Paris, and breakfasts on a slice of cold beef, English bread, and a pewter mug of ale, averring that it is superior to anything in France. He who makes this statement is called by his countrymen a *poseur.* The English race-horse is responsible for this affectation, for it was unknown before the quadruped came over the Channel.

There are other *restaurants à la carte,* which might be called third-class, where a dinner may be had for four or five francs, and here the gourmet stops. He will descend to nothing inferior to this, unless necessity compels him. If he enters a restaurant where the dinner is already prepared at a fixed price, it is because he is forced to it, as the vessel is driven into any port in a storm. But the *prix fixe* establishment, with its bill of fare chalked out on blackboard hanging outside to tempt the eye, has charms for many English and Americans. The gourmet would sooner have a good soup, one dish, and a bit of cheese, with suitable wine — the *sine qua non* of dinner — than the whole *menu* of the best repast at a fixed price. But many prefer cheap quantity to dear quality; and the restaurants of specified rate are large and usually crowded. The prices range from one to four francs, and it is singular how much is given for the money. Those ranging from two to two and a half francs do the largest business, and abound in the Passages and the Palais Royal. They are frequented by Frenchmen generally from necessity, and by foreigners of a certain kind from choice. He whose prandial joys have been confined to corn bread and pork finds difficulty in ordering a dinner; and here he finds it ready to his mouth, and as good as elsewhere: nay, he will stoutly hold that it is equal to anything in the Café Anglais. The bill of fare is a flourish of trumpets which promises much, and to him whose lights are dim the promises are fulfilled. When the disciple of Brillat-Savarin, lounging through the Passage Jouffroy, looks down through the glass doors on such a one in the act of eating, he is constrained for the time, although a good Catholic, to believe in Darwin's account of the origin of man.

The sagacious striker of oil, with his numerous family, has not been long in the Grand Hôtel before he discovers, from his point of view, that the table d'hôte dinner of the hotel can be had for half the money outside, in *a prix fixe* establishment; and, as soon as he makes the discovery, he abandons the table d'hôte, and resorts regularly — except when drawn from time to time to an Anglo-American place after his national nourishment — to a place

like the "Diners de Paris," where all sorts of things are furnished
at four francs. Here, as Miss Petrolia — the eldest of the family
group—writes home to her friends, they regale themselves on the
best Paris affords, and the bill of fare is enclosed with the letter.
The blandishments of such a repast were never heard of in the
vicinity of Oil Creek, and fill the souls of Miss Petrolia's friends
with envy. The celerity* with which papa, mamma, and the pro-
geny dispose of the courses at first astonishes the waiter, but he
is too polite to betray it in his face. He wins his way to their
hearts. As soon as he sees them coming, he tells his brother white
aprons that his Hurons have arrived; and he hurries forward with
a polite smile, hangs up their effects, and bolsters up the smaller
members of the family to a level with the table. This Machiavel
of the napkin studies their tastes, and succeeds in comprehending
something of their language, for tips are at stake. The oil-striker
is restricted to a few distorted words; but according to him his
children have enjoyed wonderful opportunities in the way of
acquiring the language, and he mainly depends on them for extended observation in ordering one of each of the several kinds
which are recorded on the well-filled bill of fare. On these occasions Miss Petrolia is usually the mouthpiece of the group, and,
with the *aplomb* which the conscious possession of a pure accent
gives, asks, among other things, for ray au bur noir, pooray de
pommes-de-terre, vol an vong, chewflur, and fromage de
roachfort, to which papa adds, with a knowing look, —
     "And a bottle of that bong Maydoek."
     And to which a little oil-striker superadds, —
     "Et vous ne forgetterez pas la crême à la glace, garçong."
     All of which the disciplined mind of the waiter carries faithfully
into the kitchen and the wine-cellar.
     They are happy. They shine in the plumes and ribbons of the
Rue de Caire, the garments of the Belle Jardinière, and the

---

* Swiftness of movement.

sparkling jewels of the Palais Royal, — all brand new; and they sit around a table served in a manner which Oil Creek in the wildest flight of its fancy could never imagine.

A three-years' residence in the posthumous city of good Americans brings modification in the group, and furnishes proof of a certain kind of adaptability in transatlantic people. The three-years' varnish of this kind of civilization unfits them for further residence on the shores of Oil Creek, and does not prepare them for the civilization which belongs to healthful life. The genuine patriotism which once burned in the breasts of the oil-strikers, and armed them against foreign criticism, becomes lukewarm. Everything American, to the saleratus* biscuit and molasses of Oil Creek, was once valiantly upheld and defended. In the fulness of their new wisdom they now tell Oil-Creekers that they know nothing of living, and cast slurs on the ancient friends of their palate, the hot bread and the old treacle. It is true, they have got beyond dinners at a fixed price, and the showy garments of the Belle Jardinière; but it is doubtful if their new, garish life gives them an equivalent for that which blessed them in the region of oil. They are doomed to a chrysalis which will not develop into the butterfly, nor return to its original form. The elders naturally have their hours of nostalgia, — especially the head of the family, when he sighs after the old days where he dropped in of an evening, without ceremony, on a fellow oil-striker, and partook of the memorable chicken stew and flannel cakes, and talked to appreciative ears of naphtha, pumps, and wells.

Turning from the oil prince to the man in blouse in the Faubourg Saint Antoine, one sees how one of the poorest classes of the great city lives. Here, of course, one cannot expect to find either the nourishment or the manners of the Montmorencys. In this repast, the soup may lack in delicacy of flavor, but it is strong

---

* A white soluble compound that is used in effervescent drinks and in baking powders and as an antacid.

and nourishing; the leg of mutton may smell greatly of garlic, but it is well cooked; the wine may have the raspiness of newness, but it has body; the lettuce may be a trifle old and wilted, but it is dressed cunningly with fair proportions of oil and other ingredients. The gestures and words of the man in blouse, as he addresses himself to these things, are naturally not those which grace the dining-room of a dwelling in the Faubourg Saint Germain. After drinking his last glass of wine, he not unfrequently turns up the glass so that the rim rests on his thumb-nail, to show that the libation has been conscientious, — *rubis sur l'ongle,* — exhibiting the last drop on the nail.

In animated accounts or stories, he often introduces his thumb-nail under the front teeth, the fingers closed, to signify "nothing whatever," usually accompanied with the words, "pas ça." To call especial attention, he places his forefinger alongside his nose, which goes with such a phrase as "Remarquez bien une chose;" and, when he shakes the same forefinger before him with a horizontal gesture, it is a negative movement, equivalent to "No, no — nothing of the kind." When in narrating he arrives at a point in his personal history where he thinks he conducted himself worthily, he rises to his feet, draws up his head, folds his arms, and fixes a penetrating look on his listener; which may be regarded as the fit attitude to the word "glorious." In moments of unusual expansion and forgetfulness, he will rub the back of his head with one hand, and at the same time dart the other back and forth in front, on a level with the eye. There is a grotesque buffoonery about this performance, which seems to have no especial signification, is considered vulgar, and its cradle is in the Faubourg Saint Antoine. When the inhabitant of this quarter essays to shine in a gallant way, he lards his speech with such words as "gracieuseté," "beau sexe," "belle dame," and the like. At a ball, in inviting a woman to dance, he has been known to say, "Voulez-vous en *suer* une, avec moi, madame?" which implies that the dancing is of a terrible vigor. Over his table he is given to the broad pun, which comes within easy range of his intelligence, and gallant allusions to the "beau sexe," — as, indeed, all Frenchmen are. This man, on the lowest round of the social ladder as he may be, does not quickly eat his dinner in silence, but prepares, as soon as he sits down, to talk as much as to eat; and anything, trivial or passing, becomes a theme of animated discussion.

Some years ago a wealthy butcher of the name of Duval established in the ordinary and inferior quarters of Paris large restaurants à la carte, which bear his name. They differ from others in having the food cooked on the furnace in the restaurant before the eyes of the client, who is thus enabled to guarantee himself against fraud. He is waited on by women, as men entail too much expense. Cheapness and cleanliness are the leading features. The restaurants are well ventilated, gayly frescoed, and the tables are of marble, usually intended for two or four. The bill of fare is handed to the client as soon as he is seated, and whatever he orders is marked thereon by the waiter. As he passes out, he stops at the counter, and pays according to the card thus marked. As politeness is found here in every class of life, the first act of the Frenchman when he enters this place, or any other restaurant, is to raise his hat to the woman of the counter, who returns his salutation with nod and smile; and in going out there is the same exchange of civilities.

There is another kind of restaurant, frequented by the very poor, which is called the *crémerie,* much inferior to the Duval establishment, with but little difference of price. The creamery is generally small, badly ventilated, and rather dirty.

As a rule, all the restaurants are prepared for the Friday fast in what the church permits her children to eat. One cannot refrain from smiling at what is called a maigre repast, consisting often of oysters, a vegetable soup, two kinds of fish, one of which is with mayonnaise, truffles, a salad of eggs, a salad of lettuce and cheese, with wine and coffee. In fidelity to such a dinner every Friday there is salvation. Thus the rich man who eats it may be saved, and the poor man, hungry through labor, and without the means to purchase such delicacies, is lost for consuming three ounces of salt pork. In a word, there is no fast for the rich, and one that lasts all the year round for the poor.

Of vegetarians from taste there are none, of those from necessity few. Lamartine was brought up as a vegetarian by his mother, who, in order to estrange him the more completely from animal food, took him to the abattoirs to see the cattle slaughtered. Until well up in his teens he did not touch flesh, but at length gave way to the general custom, and ate like his fellows not, as he alleges, that it was a matter of taste, or that he was any better for it, but rather out of compliance with the rules of society. Thus we are allowed to infer that a turnip furnished the same pleasure and nutriment to the poet as a roasted capon.

Tolerable food comes within reach of the very poor. A paper of freshly fried potatoes, which cabmen are so often seen eating on their stands while waiting for customers, costs but one or two sous.* An Auvergnat—usually a water-carrier or charcoal-burner—frequently makes his dinner of a piece of Brie cheese (the best and cheapest in the world, as pronounced at the Great Exposition of Paris by a committee of mixed nationalities) at two sous, a bit of garlic at one sou, two sous of wine, and a great piece of bread for two more; making a total of seven sous for a repast which it would be safe to affirm could not be had in any other great city, of a like quality, for a like sum. These four articles of food are wholesome, contain the essential qualities of nourishment, and are within the means of the poorest. There are few, however, who are forced to make a dinner like this every day. The Saint Antoine quarter is one of the poorest in the city; yet, when one enters into

* A sou is a French coin of low denomination; sous is the plural.

its dingy precincts, the nostrils are saluted with the savory odor of the pot-au-feu, before the dinner hour, on every side. After the bread — which is eaten in greater quantities than in any other country—the soup is the best feature of the French kitchen. What our poor people throw away in bones, scraps, and vegetables, is converted by them into nourishing soup. The waste of the American kitchen would be regarded by them as something sinful, and that which is abandoned to scavengers by a well-to-do American family would suffice to nourish a poor French one. Whatever the teeth will not go through, bone or gristle, goes into the pot, where it is boiled for hours, and made palatable with those herbs of which every French woman has such complete knowledge. Poverty may force the French housewife to buy the cheap, tough meat; but with that favorite instrument, the *casserole,* she will overcome its obdurate texture and sinews, and reduce it to a pulpy tenderness. The saucepan is her principal auxiliary, and nothing in the way of flesh can resist it.

One of the chief aids to economy in the kitchen may be traced to the facility offered in buying the exact quantity required, and no more, of meat or vegetables, at any hour of the day or evening, in the green-groceries and *charcuterie* shops found in almost every square of Paris. The *charcutier* is provided with pâtés de foie gras, Strasbourg sausages, and other articles ready for the table, and prepares chops, truffled meat, game, and meat of most kinds for the fire; when the housewife has but to light her charcoal, and cook her repast. If this be not quick enough, she may repair to the *rôtisseur,* — found also in every part of Paris, — where chickens, ducks, and pheasants are always turning on a great spit before a blazing charcoal fire, and obtain what she may require for immediate consumption. Thus, within a few doors, all that is necessary for the preparation of a generous repast may be had at once, in quantity and quality to suit, such as charcoal, wine, bread, cheese, coffee, nuts, pâtés, fruits, meats, and vegetables.

The poorest class in the United States is well-to-do compared with the poorest in France, yet it is not as well fed nor as happy. There is a general cheerfulness in this people which strikes the foreigner as soon as he enters the country. Race and climate have doubtless something to do with it, but hygienic nourishment and a sound stomach much more. In presence of this fact, one cannot help regretting the waste of time and energy of reformers and philanthropists who, to bring about man's amelioration with us, are always addressing themselves to his head, to the neglect of his stomach. It is an elementary law governing the human system, that the brain and the stomach are two neighbors who cannot afford to be at enmity any length of time without mutual deterioration, and that an improvement in the condition of one implies an improvement in the other. Naturally, this A B C knowledge is familiar to most people, but it does not yet receive the consideration which its importance demands. The foundation of the Frenchman's happiness is laid in the best bread in the world both in taste and nutriment, the most nourishing wine, and the best cooking, — save in roast beef, in the preparation of which, as well as in carving, the English enjoy a superiority. Besides the quality of the Frenchman's food, there is a healthful feature in the usually well-ventilated apartments in which it is eaten, and another in the jocularity and leisure attending the repast. Sloppy coffee and hot biscuits are not conductive to gayety; ice-cold water and thin soup peppered to the burning point are not joke-inspiring; and a potpourri of water-reeking vegetables is not productive of a humor to set the table in a roar. These, in a word, — to say nothing of those enemies of the American table, heat and haste, — are joy-killers, with sequent dyspepsia[*].

When the Frenchman in a café puts two of the little slabs of white sugar in his coffee, and the remaining two in his pocket, it is not really meanness, but economy. The four consecrated to the

[*] Resulting indigestion.

demitasse are paid for; and the purchaser may carry them home to the canary-bird, present them to the children of the concierge as a means of maintaining pleasant relations with that person, or keep them for eau sucrée. Life is not large as in the United States, where there is elasticity in the incomes. Here they are fixed; so much a year, month, and day. The line about the budget of expense is rigid, especially in the case of small rentiers, who abound in France. The man of three thousand francs a year rides on the top of the omnibus for three sous; reads the papers in one of the small reading-rooms for four sous; smokes one or two sous' worth of Caporal tobacco a day, in a pipe; goes to the theatre once a week for three to five francs, and to the café chantant once or twice, where his *consommation* costs him ten sous each time; he eats two-franc dinners, followed by that indispensable black coffee for six sous, with one or two sous gratuity, at one of the second-class cafés. The chief part of his time he strolls on the boulevards, looking in at the windows or the people, — never failing under any circumstances to admire a pretty woman, — and in sitting in the public gardens, all of which is gratuitous pleasure. The man of five thousand francs enlarges this programme; but the bachelor of twelve thousand wants for nothing. This sum means a snug little apartment of two rooms on a street running to one of the favorite boulevards, with *palissandre* furniture, each room under the glamour of one color, — pale rose, sunset beams, azure sky, or what not; some good books, a few fine engravings, perhaps a moderately good oil picture, a bit of bric-à-brac in the way of bronze and porcelain; a breakfast of three or four francs, and a dinner of five to ten francs, at the Café Riche, Vochette, or the club; cabs, theatres, Bois de Boulogne, and kid gloves at discretion. This is the definition of twelve thousand francs, for a bachelor. Twenty-five thousand, for a bachelor, is an apartment in the Boulevard Malesherbe, au second, with a cook and a man-servant, a horse and coupé, a box at the French Opera, breakfasts at home, and dinners at the Imperial or Jockey Club; the dwelling consisting of five rooms, with objects of art, one or two of some value. Fifty thousand represents an apartment au premier, with horses, carriages, valet, footman, *cordon bleu,* a wine-cellar, a box at the Italian Opera, dinners at home with friends to eat them, the usual art bibelots, a small gallery of paintings, and a good library; everything that man requires in bachelorhood. If any of these single men were doubled with a wife, the expenses would be trebled, perhaps more,—the wants of women being an unknown quantity. The man of fifty thousand would have to live, at least, like him of twenty-five, and he in turn like him of ten thousand; which, according to Frenchmen, is the explanation and the justification of the dowry system which prevails in France.

In the way of private fortune, the lowest round of the ladder is reached when he who has fifteen hundred francs a year signs himself rentier, and lives on it. These poor rich men are found in the old-fashioned pensions of the Batignolles, in the vicinity of the Jardin des Plantes, and outside the barrière, where they pay from ninety to a hundred francs a month for board and lodging, both of a meagre description. They are generally elderly people whose principal happiness consists in sitting on those benches provided by a parental government everywhere on the boulevards and in the public gardens. They are subscribers to the "Petit Journal,"— one sou, — where they carefully follow the story of unparalleled love and deep-dyed murder carried on for months in small instalments. In the public squares and the interior strips of park on some of the boulevards, they patronize the open-air performances of the cunning juggler and the spangled tumbler. They are rarely seen out of their own quarter, and their life is a round of vegetation. "Charivari" gives a sketch of two of these seedy old creatures sunning themselves on one of the hospitable benches of the Batignolles. One, striving hard to impress the other with his importance, says:

"The great general spoke to me at the review of the troops."

"Is it possible! What did he say to you?"

"He said — he said — ahem, 'Get out of the way, imbecile.'"

As a rule, every man and woman in France understands something about cooking. Many in America know how it ought to be done, but here they know how to do it. There are amateur cooks who sometimes vie with the professional cooks in preparing a good dinner. Alexandre Dumas, the elder, took more pride in the production of some of his pet dishes than of the "Count of Monte Cristo"; and has been known, when the conversation turned upon his novels, to direct it obstinately to the culinary channel, saying, "Laissons tout cela de côté, et dîtes-moi plutôt des nouvelles de ce ragoût que j'ai fait." There are few Frenchmen, who, in case of necessity, would not be able to cook their own dinner. The French women enjoy the same facility in the preparation of food that they do in making robes and hats. They may not exercise their faculties in these directions from being in a condition of life which enables them to employ others; but the latent capacity is there, like a second nature.

In the summer time it is the desire of every Parisian to dine in the open air; and between six and seven in the evening the garden restaurants of the city are full of clients. In the environs, the restaurants by border of lake and stream present an equally animated appearance well into the night; and here, in cleverly arranged bosquets, in groves, or under vine-clad lattice-work, the Parisians vivaciously dine. For the time the occupation of the city is forgotten: there is but one thing in the world to be done; and it is to eat, drink, and be merry. The mustache-pointed, waist-pressed soldier fights his battles over again; and the old bald-headed gallant, such as Gavarni loved to draw, tells of the desperate raids he made in the heart of woman in his younger days. One Gallic Werther murmurs a page or two of his romantic past, while another rhapsodizes over the present. Octave warmly pleads his cause over the table, and the sportive maiden confesses that she loves him. It is a rural Babel and one of Watteau's pictures thrown together, with a running accompaniment of clattering forks and clinking glasses; and, over all, intermittent cries of "Garçon," with responsive shouts of "Le voilà, le voilà — à l'instant même."

For those of adequate means the restaurants embowered in the park of Vincennes, or the well-known Madrid in the heart of the Bois de Boulogne, offer great attractions. Here come the winter and fall clients of the Café Anglais and the Trois Frerès, and seat themselves, at a late dining hour, in a brilliantly lighted bower, where the ear is pleased with trickling fountains, and the eye with soft-globed lights shining down on graceful statues relieved on night-green backgrounds. This is the spot preferred by *the princesse de la rampe* with her following of foolish swells, where she orders the lobster and champagne style of dinner, which her admirers count it a privilege to pay for. Here, with a glass of the Rheims nectar in her hand, she pronounces *mots* which sparkle before the mental vision of her audience with pyrotechnic brightness, and sings the music of Offenbach with a grimace and gesture which set the table in a roar. The princess is rated irresistible. Will her highness be crowned with flowers? Will she be raised on a pedestal? Will she take another glass of champagne? Singular question the last! Was she ever known to refuse? "Il fait toujours *soif* chez moi — versez, mes enfants." *Renversante!* Will the princess sing that divine song again? The *bis* runs around the table, and her highness deigns when the performance is received with renewed applause. "Vive la princesse!" Will she sit on a sultanic throne with a crowd of worshippers at its base? Will she take another piece of lobster? She deigns, for "il fait toujours *faim* chez elle." And all this is garnished with inimitable gestures of hand and foot, in the manner of the Duchess of Gerolstein.

To cool heads the dinner with the princess is somewhat threadbare, having already been served in theatres and journals; but the foolish swells do not have cool heads, and the farce goes on without abatement the summer through.

The bucolic restaurant of Jules the student and Léontine the shop-girl in its simplicity is very different from the magnificence of the Madrid. A coarse cloth, but white as snow, covers their rustic table; the soup is of the old pot-au-feu kind, which will never go out of fashion as long as there are healthy palates to appreciate it; a tender radish or two, a good Chateaubriand, "lez-z-z haricots verts," as the facetious call them; Brie cheese, a bottle or two of fair Bordeaux, coffee, the petit verre, and these two dine, as Jules puts it, like a pope. The enjoyment of a Trois Frères dinner is not superior to this simple repast, for Jules and Léontine eat with an appetite. Under the pleasing stimulant of food and wine, Jules, of course, does not neglect such an occasion to inform Léontine, perhaps for the hundredth time, and in a dozen different forms, of his undying love, which the reciprocative Léontine prizes as much as the dinner, and this is saying much. The running fire of tender babble is long sustained; and, when she asks who loves Titine, the question draws the fire of a volley of declarations from the ever-ready Jules. "Pas vrai." Soft, sinless Gallic oaths attest to the truth. How much does he love her? "Tout plein — tout plein. Et toi donc, Titine?" — "Ah je t'aime bien, va." And, when the fair and fond Titine is asked if she will ever cease to love her Jules, it elicits the grand "Jamais," repeated like an echo.

To a third party there may be tiresome repetition in this scene, if heard more than once; but to this tender twain it is always fresh, and palpitating with interest. In these moments of prandial expansion, to her lover's eyes Léontine is, of course, a goddess incarnate with grace and beauty; and, to her, Jules is something Olympian, with an aureole about his head. After the repast there is reclining on the grass, where Léontine sits with that lovely masculine head in her lap, fondling with the hair; or there is lounging through the forest, where the twain gather flowers, and where the grisette pulls off the petals of the marguerite, accompanied with the sacramental words, "Il m'aime un peu, beaucoup, passionnément, pas du tout," to assure herself of Jules's eternal affection. Or Jules takes out his brier pipe and tobacco pouch, — worked by the lovely hands of the only woman in the world, — and whiffs at the Caporal, while perhaps the naughty Léontine does the same with a cigarette, to place herself à la hauteur de la situation, as they leisurely lounge together, forgetful of everything in this busy world but themselves.

Their gayety is apt to take the form of song; and, if veined with sentiment, the old, old story, as told for the people by one of them, their most gifted poet, Béranger, is sung with a fine expression of that wit and pathos which the songster knew so well to mingle together. If there are two or three Léontines and as many Jules, a livelier gayety rules the hour. Then the notes of Offenbach and Hervé are wafted through the trees with chorus of voice and clink of glass. King Blague presides. A *blagueur* snatches up a walking stick, in guise of a guitar, and twangs imaginary strings under fictive window in burlesque serenade. Another, with goblet of Mephistopheles in outstretched hand and curious grimace, caricatures the "Veau d'Or." Nothing is sacred; and the "Marsellaise," with its soul-stirring spirit, is turned into ridicule with imitation of drum refrains and gestures of drum-major that would move the most melancholy man to mirth. Trumpets are created out of field-stalks, and the ra-ta-tah is given in imitation of the pet trumpeters of his late majesty, the instruments to one side, and elevated after the manner of the originals, in broadest burlesque.

The compatriots of Jules and Léontine are the inheritors of savory food and toothsome wine. For several hundred years they have been the leading gastronomers. The glories of the kitchen passed from Rome to France; and, although the eagle may now be down, the spit is still aloft. The person who handled this emblem of his office two hundred years ago was an authority that might not be disputed with impunity. Under Louis XIV. was developed that punctilious honor which led Vatel to fall on his suicidal sword like a Roman of the olden time. Mme. de Sévigné tells how the failure of the fish drove him to his chamber, where he spitted himself like a turkey, and thus embalms the memory of the kitchen Cato in history for all time.

In the times of the Regency and Louis XV., he who created a new dish deserved well of his country, and the genius of invention was unceasingly at work in the kitchen. Dandies and fashionable women entered the lists with the professional man in white, and cudgelled their brains to invent sauces, as men now do to invent labor-saving machines.

These were what the man in white would call the good old times, when a *cordon bleu* kept his carriage, and his society was courted by princes of the blood; when men lived to eat, and dining out was a profession; but he must admit, however good these times were for him, they were bad for the state, and that whenever he reached his apotheosis, in Rome, Athens, or Alexandria, it was the mark of the decadence of the nation. This fact is not as pleasant to swallow as one of his succulent dishes; but it is well for Monsieur le Cuisinier to take and digest it, in order to better understand his mission, which should limit itself to the hygienic, and to the rejection of the superfluous and the artificial. He cannot evade the responsibility: he is to some extent accountable for the downfall of nations. With his seductive *plats* and wines he helped on the road to ruin the frail Egyptians and sybaritic Greeks, and destroyed the stern virtues of Roman warriors. At his inspiration Alexander committed the follies of the table in the guise of Mercury or Jupiter, and Mark Antony arrayed himself in the sparse garments of Bacchus, and revelled in the pleasures of the god whom he portrayed, in a theatre of Athens, before a public audience. At his prompting, Cleopatra, in shameless paucity of dress, presided at extravagant feasts, destroyed the idea of royal virtue in the public mind, and softened the heads of great Roman conquerors. The man in white, like an evil genius, was in at the death of the Babylonians, and of the dissolute inhabitants of Ephesus and Antioch. He is especially open to censure in the part he played in the feasts of the Roman decadence, where the greatest men of the time fell into drunkenness and gluttony; and one cannot help thinking that in Hades these Luculus feasts must lie heavy on the conscience of him who was the presiding genius of the terrible *dégringolade.* The Egyptian cook, under similar circumstances, may find a grain of comfort in the fact, that, previous to the extravagant repasts to which he administered, he caused a small coffin, containing an ivory skeleton, to be carried around, and shown to each guest, signifying, "You will one day be like this: enjoy yourself while you may." Thus grave admonition was implied in this lugubrious[*] exhibition; but the Roman cook let his people go to their doom without a single warning.

Under the Second Empire there was possibly a tendency in Paris to follow in the footsteps of old Rome. Natural and factitious forces conspired to create wealth, prodigality prevailed, and virile, intellectual life was in danger of being destroyed in the material. The kitchen man of Regency days had made his appearance, and was beginning to make the *plats* of ancient days. But the war and the dynastic overthrow arrested the movement in this direction; and Paris, giant, reckless, and reeling, has been sobered by misfortune, and the healthful discipline of a new era. A long carnival has been gone through with; and now, doubtless, lost forces will be recovered, at least for a time, in the Lenten season of republicanism.

---

[*] Exaggerated, affected or excessive mournfulness.

CHAPTER 4

A Day with the Painters

THE STUDIO of X—— was at the upper end of the Luxembourg Garden; the walls were of that bluish gray affectioned by most painters; and the light was broad and soft. With him were two women-models, one of whom had been posing. They were both dressed; one was just completing her toilet. The easel bore an unfinished picture of Pelagia in an attitude of meditation tinder an olive-tree. The painter, serious and humorous by turns, like most Frenchmen, explained his subject in characteristic speech.

"As you are doubtless aware," said he, "Pelagia was a celebrated actress in Antioch, known as the *Pearl,* who turned the heads of many foolish young men, as well as those of some old wise ones; in a word, the Schneider of Antioch theatricals. In the midst of her gay life and mundane triumphs, she hears a sermon by Bishop Gregorius, a celebrated preacher, whose eloquence brings about her conversion. In my picture I endeavor to seize the moment when the change of heart begins. As you see, she seeks solitude, and is reclining under an olive-tree in a posture of melancholy reflection. To bring out the traits of Pelagia, I employ two models, one for the face and the other for the figure. As you have been in Palestine, please tell me if my olive-tree is after nature."

As I had often sat under the old olive-trees of the Garden of Gethsemane and the Valley of Jehoshaphat, under which Pelagia had also doubtless many times reclined, I was able to give a fair idea of their appearance. This elicited serious discussion from him for five or ten minutes; when, turning to the models, who were on the point of going, he said: "Conduct yourselves wisely, my dear Pelagias, and you will be happy. Recollect that you are now butterfly saints who have emerged from the chrysalis of theatrical depravity which once existed in the festive town of Antioch. I shall expect you at your respective hours tomorrow; let no pleasure junketing interfere with your appointment."

After the departure of the young women, the painter went with me to an atelier on the other side of the Seine, where students drew from the model in classes, and on the way spoke of the theory of judging of the appearance of men after their work, and by way of illustration, to show that there was no foundation for the theory, referred to Gérôme. His older works, the "Gladiateurs," the "Mort de César," and "Phryné devant le Tribunal," as well as one of his later, "Cléopatre," suggested a pagan taste; and his genre pictures, like the "Duel après le Bal," indicated a mundane dramatic character. In a word, his work exhibited a certain sublimated materialism which would lead one to expect in him a Parisianized Oriental, full of sensuous tastes; when, in point of fact, he was a slight, pale man, with large, melancholy brown eyes, and features of perfect purity of outline, — a chastened spirit, one would say, full of charity to all mankind; a monk of the studio, working sadly but steadfastly in expiation of the sins of others. Meissonier, seen through works like the "Attente," the "Lecture chez Diderot," the "Capitaine," the "Corps de Garde," suggested a solitary artist in artistic apparel living in Bohemia, who disliked the Philistine spirit of today, and systematically shut himself in the sixteenth and eighteenth centuries, and who, with a horror of the tastes and habits of the bourgeoisie, lived in regions unknown to it, — a lonely, picturesque man in sack coat and slouch hat. Meissonier in reality was a dapper, red-faced man, who wore the shiniest of silk hats, and resembled more than anything else that bourgeois from whom he fled as from the wrath to come. In the works of Bouguereau there was a poetical sadness which indicated a pale student of nature; while in the flesh he was a jolly, red-cheeked, plump little man, full of gayety, — especially pleased with Americans because they bought his pictures. There was none of the grotesque humor of Gustave Doré's drawings in his face nor his manner, and he might be taken for almost anyone but a painter. That consummate master of drawing who delighted in painting Arab scenes — Boulanger — presented nothing in his appearance either for or against the probability of the authorship of his work: he was a thin, sallow-faced little man, of pleasant expression, and a head entirely bald with the exception of three stiff little sprouts of hair, which were always wide awake and unyielding. Lefebvre, as regarded the identification of personality with work, occupied the same neutral ground, — a youngish man, quick and decided in speech and movement, with large blue eyes, and slightly bald; all of which had nothing to do with his exquisite manner of painting woman's form. There was one, however, who looked exactly like his work, namely, Cabanel; by exception, to prove the rule against the theory, a stately, courteous man, with hair and beard almost white, and, in striking contrast to them, dark eyes and eyebrows. Most of his personal characteristics were found in his pictures. In his work of the "Naissance de Vénus" there was elegance, purity, and beauty of lines and modelling, and that sombreness in coloring which he always employed; the purity almost attained to coldness. His portraits were posed in a grand way, elegantly draped. These qualities were all singularly like the man.

Our arrival at the atelier cut short further discussion of the subject; and we mounted a well-worn stairway of one of the old-fashioned houses alongside the Seine, to one of the upper stories.

About twenty students were here collected, awaiting the arrival of the person who was to pose. A glowing stove made the place excessively warm, with a view to the comfort of the expected model. As it was customary to admit only painters, X —— advised me not to intimate that I did not belong to the priesthood of art, as painters, and especially models, disliked the presence of Philistines—laymen being thus designated in the language of the atelier.

Presently the model arrived,—a bright, handsome brunette of nineteen or twenty. There was a demonstration of welcome from the painters, the door was locked, and she proceeded in a business-like fashion to prepare for work. When ready, she mounted a platform about two feet high, where she fell under a lofty, broad side-light. Two of the more advanced painters, who acted as a committee of arrangements, placed her in a position. This being the first pose, there was discussion about the posture to be assumed. Several times the two placed her, and then retired a few yards to observe the effect, remarking as they did so, "Don't hold the arm so stiff," "Incline the head a trifle," and what not, accompanied with painter's pantomime, such as slowly sawing the head, shutting out portions with the intercepted hand, and massing the effects with half-closed eyes. The fourth trial proved to be a success, at which a phrase of general satisfaction was expressed. The two, enjoining her not to budge, with the others got behind their easels, and event to work, some taking off their coats. One modelled in clay: with this exception all held crayons. All the faces turned earnestly toward the canvas, the clay, and the model, and not a sign of dawdling or frivolity was to be seen. To them the woman was a statue. Nothing was recognized here but art: it took the form of worship, and he who looked with other eyes than those of an artist was accounted sacrilegious. Thus the public opinion of the atelier made them all artists; and, if the art feeling was not possessed, it was assumed.

After a time the silence was broken by her requesting someone to heat up the stove as she was cold, which brought out one or two ejaculations, and a murmur that we were already in the interior of Africa; to which she retorted that, they would not think so if they were in her place. Another long silence was interrupted by her asking the time, at which one of the elders remarked, "Not yet; mademoiselle." Again, in a few minutes she said she was sure the time must be up. "It is, my child," answered the same elder: "repose yourself." She left the stand, drew a mantle about her, and took a seat by the stove with a sense of relief. She was obliged to look out for herself in regard to the time of posing, as the painters were usually so absorbed as to forget it.

The repose of the model brought with it a contrast to the previous silence. There was a general buzz, and lighting of pipes and cigarettes. Two or three compliments were addressed to the model for her excellent posing; native gallantry cropped out, and two or three told her she was an angel or a duchess, to which she replied in that spirit of raillery with which these things were uttered. This was an illustration of French character, — fond of work, and equally fond of play.

I approached the model as she sat by the stove, and entered into conversation with her, when I learned that she had another occupation, that of artificial flower maker, by which she earned three francs a day. Posturing was naturally more profitable; she received five francs for the two hours and a half to three hours she remained in the atelier, during which she posed about two hours, the remainder being taken up in rests. The times of repose she called her *entr'actes*. Believing me to be a painter, she called my attention, in a simple, natural way, to the roundness of her arm, the texture and color of the skin, and the curved lines of her shoulder. She went on to say in a manner purely professional, —

"My arms and shoulders are my best points, and I occasionally pose for them: I like it much better than posing for the whole figure."

At length the painter in authority told her it was time to resume the pose, and before stepping on the platform she looked at his watch. She was posing for Cynthia, who cast the shepherd Endymion into a deep sleep in order to kiss him. One of the painters having acquainted her with the mythological story of the artful stealing of the osculation, she observed that she paid very little attention to such nonsense,—besides, one could not believe more than half of what these painters said about such things. Then she fell cleverly into the posture, guided by a few directions. As they proposed to work on the face, she was instructed to wear a pleased expression. Cynthia was taken at the moment she is advancing toward the sleeping Endymion to snatch the kiss, coy, and yet impelled by sweet temptation.

"Try, my child," said the man in authority, "to imagine that the young man you love is lying asleep before you, with his pockets full of bank-notes."

This had the desired effect: the model could not help laughing, and the traces of it remained some time on her face. All fell to work again, and silence was supreme, as each tried to transfer Cynthia's happy face to canvas. Once in a while, when, through lassitude or forgetfulness, she modified the posture, *papa* — the elder painter — said to her sharply, "Mademoiselle, pay attention"; which showed that, however much license was allowed during the rests, rigid discipline was exacted in time of work.

When she got through, she made her toilet in the same business-like way that she had unmade it. She asked for a looking-glass to complete it, but the article could not at once be found. "What savages!" said she; "twenty men, and not one mirror! But I am not surprised at it: you are such monsters you are afraid to look at yourselves." As Frenchmen like to be called monsters by the women, this was taken as a general compliment. At length a cracked mirror — poetically styled *starred* — was produced, before which she smoothed out her plumage like a bird in the sunshine. Her attire was simple: a sombre-colored little hat, black alpaca robe, dark brown mantle, closely fitting gloves and boots, and a parasol in hand, comprised her costume. Equipped, she had the demeanor of a *rosière* of Nanterre, or a convent girl.

The five-franc piece was handed to her enveloped in paper, a mark of delicacy. After making an appointment for another day, she passed out with a modest, quiet air, amidst a general chorus of adieus.

The painters soon followed the model, except three who remained behind to select other models. X —— as one of these, which permitted me also to remain. The trio discussed the defects, as well as the *points,* in the flowerist who had just left, after which it was decided that another model was necessary to complete their Cynthia. They also expressed a desire to have a man to pose for Samson; and, as they were talking about it, such a one, amongst others, presented himself. He said that he had achieved success as John the Baptist and Ajax; he averred that he was even strong enough to do the Laocoön. He was requested to strip, which he did with despatch. He was a man of extreme masculine development, looking like a prize-fighter of the heavy weights. He was placed in several postures which brought out the muscles like cords; and whilst going through these attitudes he called attention to his points: "There is a leg for you, messieurs, —strong enough to support the façade of the Madeleine. And this breast, —you might break stones on it. I beg you to examine the arm, a bundle of ropes twisted together—quoi"

The Ajax was going on in this strain, when he was interrupted by one of the painters, who told him he had too much of one thing. On his asking what that was, he was informed that it was tongue.

"That is a bad foot you have there, my friend," remarked a painter.

"There is nothing the matter with it, monsieur."

"One of the bones is gone. How did you lose it?"

"What an eye monsieur has! A surgeon took it out after an accident."

It required a practised eye to note this slight malformation; but these painters, trained in anatomy like surgeons, were not long in discovering it. As soon as the model learned that he was to be engaged to pose for Samson, he said that he had done it before, and with remarkable success. Showing his brawny arms, he asked if they did not also want something else; he was up to the requirements of the Fighting Gladiator, or anything in that line. I ventured to inquire which gladiator; and he replied, as one who recited an often-told tale, —

"He of the Louvre, a pugilist: antique, brown with age; attitude leaning forward; left hand raised on guard, right hand thrown out back ready to strike a side-blow; right leg bent; straight line from the head to the toe of left foot; muscles vividly revealed in intense development; a wonderful petrifaction, as if he had been smitten to stone at the instant of striking."

"How well he describes it," I observed to my companion.

"Yes: he is repeating the catalogue." After the departure of the strong man, other models made their appearance, men and women; but most of them went away without securing an engagement. The chief aim of the committee charged with the business was, to find models possessing a leading characteristic, — a laughing man, a fierce one, a noble one; a sad woman, a gay one; and so on. Naturally, a prime object of pursuit was the beautiful woman, concerning whom opinions differed somewhat, but the most general one was that she possessed abundant hair, golden or warmly-tinted light brown; a rather small head, low forehead, eyebrows delicately arched; eyes *à fleur de tête,* contrary to the idea of the ancients, who put them deep in the head; that oval outline of face which has been classic from all time; legs long, and a waist consequently short. She was a woman of chaste symmetry, the reverse of the massive woman of the old Flemish painters. It was held in the atelier, that fat destroyed the line of beauty, and robbed color of its delicate transparency, and was, in a word, the great enemy of the beautiful woman. The Grecian nose, describing a straight line to the top of the forehead, was regarded as an affectation, and therefore to be cast out of the temple of art as something pernicious, in obedience to that axiom that nothing is beautiful but the true.

In the examination of the models, there was discussion concerning the poising or balancing of the figure, the rule being that the head should be directly over the foot on which the body rests, and that in whatever direction the head turned the weighted foot should follow. Compliance with this rule brought the figure into the most natural position. If the head was thrown back to look up, the foot was moved back to conserve the equilibrium; and as the head was thrust forward there was the corresponding movement of the resting foot. The head was never to be turned without a corresponding movement of the body; the turn beginning at the neck, and descending to the waist. The head was not to be thrown back except to look up. The license in the use of arms and legs was greater, yet subject to certain formulas. The hand in any ordinary action was not to reach higher than the head, the fist higher than the shoulder, the foot higher than the knee; and in the tranquil pose the space between the feet should not exceed one foot. The sympathetic action of the body with the leading movement was never to be lost sight of; an arm is raised, and all that side of the body exhibit the same tendency, even to the heel which rises from the floor.

The key to art in the matter of posing was to have the model well poised; for it was held, that, unless there was solidity in the pose, it was unnatural. Hence the oft-repeated question to the model, "Do you feel easy?" and, to satisfy by comparison, the model was occasionally requested to take her own natural position, and say whether she felt as comfortable in the other as this one. Those who arranged the pose also put themselves in the same attitude, to discover if there was any constraint in it, and then changed it to others, to arrive at the poise by comparison, as in the case of the model. Without familiarity with the pose on the part of the model, it was impossible to get that *naïveté* of movement indispensable in a true work of art. The affectation which came from constrained position was what was most to be avoided; and the aim always in view was, not to show science in art, but nature. According to these painters, the grace and nobility of expression in the work of the ancients came to them, in great part, from simplicity of pose. Exaggeration of movement was something fraught with evil to art; and the ateliers where it was practised were referred to as the gymnasiums of contortionists, the racks of tortured models, and the homes of body-wrigglers and face-twisters.

The workers in this atelier were opposed to the representation of heightened, heroic action, designated by them as extravagant and melodramatic; and in this I think that French painters generally share their idea. The tendency of art today is toward pictures which represent repose. The age is not militant, but peaceful: no civilized people would now wage a thirty-years' war. The senses are becoming more refined, and scenes of violence more revolting; and the general desire of comfort, and a life free from perils and shocks, is finding its way into the pictures. Hence the fashion of what are called, for want of a better name, genre pictures, with the peaceful, red-hued warriors of Meissonier, and the lazy, poetical figures of Gérôme. Painters, guided by the spirit of the age, select subjects from modern life that are not of a harrowing character, — those that tell of gentle emotions and amiable sentiments, and little domestic scenes, such as the "Bénédicité," the "Prière;" and the "Bibliothèque" of Edouard Frère; the "Soeurs de Charité," the "Pharmacie," the "Toilette," and the "Consolation" of Madame Henriette Brown; and the views of luxurious life of Toulmouche and Tissot. The picture-buyers are in a great measure responsible for the genre picture, for the painter forms himself after their taste. Two hundred years ago only rich lords and

powerful princes could own pictures. Now there is general cultivation, and a desire to possess, under the restriction of certain limits
in the way of price. Besides, apartments are small, which imposes
limitation in space as well as in money, and historical pictures can
only find a place in a public gallery. Thus money, space, and the
general taste, are against the follower of Paul Delaroche. The time
is past, at least for years to come, for painting such pictures as the
"Radeau de la Méduse" of Géricault, and the "Martyre de Saint
Symphorien" of Ingres; for neither the taste of the public nor the
genius of the painters runs in this direction. The high horse of art
has been ridden so hard as to be run to death, and the mediocri-
ties who have been astride of him during the last few years has-
tened the demise. This one, like Pegasus, must be mounted by
one who knows how; otherwise he is soon overtaken with igno-
minious limp and disastrous fall. Historical art, in a word, is like
tragedy, which must be interpreted by genius; in the hands of
mediocrity it falls into that ridicule from which it is separated by
only a single step.

The genre picture has been popularized in some measure by the
excess of work in the old field. From gladiators fighting and dying, church subjects from the Holy Family through all the saints,
battles full of carnage, agony, and death, the mind now turns
away with a sense of relief, to the contemplation of the actual and
comparatively tranquil scenes of today. Richard Coeur de Lion
laying open the head of a Saracen with his terrible battle-axe does
not possess half the interest of a couple of lovers under the tryst-
ing tree. Ajax defying the lightning is not nearly as engaging as
a couple of chubby, joyous children in the midst of a flock of
poultry. The amateur remorselessly turns away from Caesar ago-
nizing under the stroke of Brutus, to dwell on Belinda reading a
declaration from her beloved. Togas, sandals, and Olympian
games have had their day, as well as the after-coming doublet and
hose, flounce and ruffle. The amateur will no longer look at the

ancient Bayard defending a bridge single-handed against hundreds; but Bayard of the nineteenth century, uttering his glib and gallant speech in a boudoir, occupies him for half an hour. He is surfeited with the flash of swords, tired of majestic Jupiters and weeping Didos, but is quickly absorbed in a child tending geese or a tatterdemalion* riding a donkey. The picture which he likes is hard to fix with a definition. Every other department of painting save this has a name which interprets clearly what it is. Thus historical, battle, religious, animal, marine, landscape, and still-life pictures have names which leave no doubt as to what they are; but *genre* is a vague designation, which covers a wide field of subjects,—something purely conventional, meaning anything from a man to an infant, or a camel to a mouse. In a desire to arrive at a closer definition, the *genre* is called by some an easel picture, which is perhaps the nearest approach that can be made to a classification. It is a small canvas which tells a simple story that almost everyone can understand, and this best suits an unheroic age.

The painters in the school alongside the Seine were affected by the vogue, as well as the amateurs who linger about Goupil's gallery, and exhibited little ambition to walk in the footsteps of Ingres and Eugène Delacroix in the regions of high art, but showed a marked tendency to follow in the field of those masters who were reaping harvests in the production of easel pictures.

There are many who think that the present fashion is injurious to art, and that the masters who confine themselves to the production of easel pictures are like composers of music who compose only pretty ballads and waltzes to the neglect of grand operas; that the grand grouping of the large picture requires the exercise of the highest faculty of the painter,—that of creation; and that the restricted use of his lesser faculties in the production

* Someone ragged or disreputable in appearance; a dirty shabbily clothed urchin.

of small simple subjects dwarfs his power. Those who favor the present movement derisively affix the word *romantic* to the pictures of such as Gros, who today would be a giant reaching head and shoulders above contemporaneous painters. And they who remain faithful to the interpretation of the grand passions are distanced in the race for honor and gain. It is the expression of the same prevalent taste which pronounces against the eloquence of the classic orator in favor of the unvarnished language of the simple talker, — which turns away from the grandeur of Mozart to the easily-comprehended airs of Auber. All the arts have undergone a change since the existence of the last empire, and that materialism which belonged to it has almost destroyed the taste for the heroic. That a certain change from the overcharged pictures of the past is a healthy sign, there is little doubt; but the *juste milieu* has been passed, as is generally the case in such movements, and the other extreme reached. The picture of Napoleon on a gray horse, galloping up the Alps, swathed in a voluminous mantle, with his face turned toward the spectator as if seeking his admiration, was mock-heroic, and is now properly condemned. On the other hand, the picture of the same subject by David, where the great captain labors up the mountain side on a led mule, his face lost in melancholy abstraction, is not appreciated at its just value, through the want of heroic sentiment. Any subject which bears a resemblance to the act of getting upon stilts, in the estimation of the majority of painters and amateurs, now meets with unqualified disapproval, and shows the remarkable reaction which has taken place.

Still occasional efforts are made by men of talent, out of the popular field, that are attended with fair results. Of these Bouguereau is one; and, of the few heroic subjects he has attempted, one of the best is the "Flight of Orestes," where the stabber of Clytemnestra is pursued by the Furies; it shows some power, and is very good in color. He has another of the same order hanging in his atelier, of a scene in the infernal regions, strong but extravagant. But these pictures must be considered rather as experiments; for the heart of Bouguereau dwells in pleasant scenes of every day, such as Italian women and children in costume.

Cabanel is generally regarded as the foremost man in the department of *romantic* art. His "Birth of Venus" has a wide reputation, but is unpleasant to me both in color and manner of treatment. Of those that I have seen, his "Nymph and the Satyr," — I am not sure of the title, — which hangs in the Luxembourg, is the best specimen of his work. The satyr has raised the nymph from the ground, and encloses her with his left arm, while his right hand firmly grasps one of her arms as she struggles for release; her head is thrown back and turned from him in horror and disgust, while her massive golden hair almost sweeps the ground. The contrast is fine between the dark-brown flesh of the monster and that of the beautiful and symmetrical woman. The satyr is crowned with scarlet poppies and green leaves, a leopard-skin hangs down from his back, and his features are relaxed by a sensual grin. The background, with far-off slaty-blue hills, is very good. Almost all painters are fond of *chiaroscuro,* ever since Rembrandt revealed its power; but Cabanel is an exception. He holds that it is not necessary to have dark shadows in order to relieve and to model, and his productions are comparatively free from them. There is so little shadow in them that the idea is suggested of a little clap-trap in making the light so artificial.

Gustave Moreau is another painter who shows an inclination to follow in the path which has been almost abandoned since the death of Ingres and Eugene Delacroix, and his pictures, the "Orphans" and the "Young Man and Death," show a rare taste and much delicacy. There are others who occasionally do this kind of work, but few or none who devote themselves entirely to it. The case is quite different with painters of religious subjects, animals, still life, &c., each one of whom, as a rule, confines himself to his special branch of art.

In the evening X —— conducted me to another atelier in the Passage Panorama, near the Boulevard des Italiens. The stairs which we mounted led up to a little room whose walls were garnished with studies in oil, and shelves upon which were placed plaster casts of various heads and figures from the antique, while in separate corners stood colossal figures of the Venus of Milo and the Venus of Medicis. One side of the room formed an arched doorway, closed by the heavy folds of a green curtain, which was pulled aside, when we came full upon a scene that to me was novel. At the further end of the atelier, on a carpeted platform, with green drapery for background, stood what I was tempted to believe was the wax figure of a woman, so motionless was she, with the numerous gas-jets, with shining reflectors behind them, directed full upon her. What first destroyed the illusion was the movement of the eyes, which began turning slowly in our direction; save in this, the woman was as immovable as a statue. The professor who had charge of the atelier was much pleased with the immobility of the pose, and said, "Perfect;" upon which a rosy wave passed from the temples of the woman over her face, and disappeared in her shoulders as her eyes grew something brighter. In looking at the model, a new consciousness of the fact was acquired, that in nature woman is the highest expression of the beautiful. As the work went on the fall of a pin might have been heard, for the professor was a rigid disciplinarian. At length he ordered a rest, when the working rules, as in the other atelier, were entirely suspended, and everyone moved about and talked as he pleased. The model drew a shawl about her person, and seated herself on the end of the platform.

The painters of this atelier were composed of both sexes, working together apparently without difficulty. Six or seven women were present, two of whom were Americans. On making the acquaintance of one of the latter she observed, —

"Some of our countrymen find an impropriety in our working in a mixed atelier, and perhaps there is, according to society's code. But, if a woman wants to be a painter, she must get over her squeamishness; if she wants to paint strong and well like a man, she must go through the same training. The trial to a modest young woman is at first great; but, as soon as she is possessed of the art feeling, the first impression which she receives on entering the atelier quickly wears away, and she is soon absorbed in her work like those around her. There is no sex here: the students, men and women, are simply painters. In the atelier, excessive modesty in a woman painter is a sign of mediocrity; only the woman who forgets the conventionalities of society in the pursuit of art stands a chance for distinction. If the woman has not a desire, an enthusiasm, to profit by the advantages of the atelier, she had better never touch paint nor pencil. This is one of the best ateliers in Paris to learn to paint in, and this is a sufficient reason for our coming here. Society can no more be governed by the rules of art, than the atelier can be governed by the rules of society. If Rosa Bonheur had occupied her time looking after the proprieties, she would not stand where she does today."

There was something almost defiant in the remarks of the young woman, as if she held a position that required defending. What she said, too, left an inference that she had broken many lances in maintaining herself on what is regarded as debatable ground.

There was posing in this atelier day and night. The models succeeded each other in alternation, — men one week, women the next, varied sometimes by little children, and even an occasional negro. Every Monday, a number of models appeared at the atelier to exhibit their good points, in the hope of being engaged by the professor. Each one, as his or her turn came, stepped on the platform, going through the various poses with the utmost gravity and decorum. It was rather a sad spectacle, as most of them had to be turned away. On this day, also, each student selected his or her place for the entire week, and the first comer had his name placed first on the list. Then came the selection of the pose, which was often a difficult matter, and consumed sometimes two or three hours, so various were the pros and cons regarding each pose; often it had to be settled by vote. As soon as the pose had been agreed upon, the first name on the list was called, the student thus summoned selected the best place from which to see the model, put his stool and easel there, and drew a chalk line on the floor around the spot, with his initials in the inside, in order to claim it in case it were appropriated by another during an accidental absence or a tardy appearance. The next student on the list selected the next best place, and so on till the end. Those who drew without painting occupied low ranges of stools immediately around the model, so as not to interfere with the view of the painters beyond them. The model posed for three-quarters of an hour, beginning a quarter after the striking of the hour, and continuing until the next striking, the succeeding quarter being occupied as a rest. As in the other atelier, the rests were devoted to amusements, the models contributing thereto as well as the students. They made caricatures of each other; if anyone manifested vexation at being caricatured, he never after had any peace, for they all drew him then, and with the most ignoble traits. A person of this kind was being burlesqued while I was present. They drew him as a jumping jack, and as a devil popping out of a box. He had a turn-up nose which was dwelt upon with an exaggeration of form that moved almost everyone to mirthfulness; the laughter of the model brought the tears to her eyes.

A fine-looking old-man model was a favorite in the atelier, and during his rests went about among the easels to criticise the work. He had been a model all his life, and had often posed for Couture, Lefebvre, Gérôme, and other noted artists; it was said his traits could be recognized in a number of their pictures. Another model, a powerful fellow who posed for the strong men, was a prestidigitator, who, during his rests, performed tricks with cards and handkerchiefs, and juggled tumblers, with the dexterity and audacity of a circus-performer. A younger model was a standing butt for having at an unfortunate moment boasted that the blood of the Périgords flowed in his veins. He was never allowed to forget it; and, when he neglected his pose, one of the young men would cry out to correct him, "'The pose, the pose!" and another would respond, "How can you expect a Périgord to mind the pose? ridiculous!" et cetera.

A number of these ateliers exist in Paris, offering facilities, not found elsewhere in the world, to all who desire to learn to paint, draw, and model in clay, in addition to the government schools in the Beaux Arts. A magnificent temple is furnished by the government for the exhibition of statues and pictures; honors are conferred on those who distinguish themselves in any branch of art. The government galleries, full of treasures in marble and canvas, are thrown open to all without price, which renders them as accessible to the poor as to the rich. Art delineation in books and journals is general and cheap. Through the fostering care of the authorities, joined to a native aptitude, the art sentiment is more generally developed than in any other country, and the evidences of it are seen in many ways. One of its common expressions is in the ordinary signs over the shops and taverns, which are often executed by men who merit the name of artists instead of signpainters. One often meets with a piece of still life over the door of an eating-house or a wine-shop equal to what hangs on the diningroom walls of an epicure. As a rule, every man is an artist in his profession, be he prime minister mounted on the theatrical tribune of the chamber, or cook in spotless white behind his glittering array of saucepans. Mantua-makers agonize over the importance of a waist a quarter of an inch too long, and head-ornamenters ponder for hours over the question of putting a rosebud or a japonica in the hair of madame the countess. The shoemaker makes a study of the feet of Monsieur Chose; and, though they should have the shape of tadpoles, they shall be hid in forms that are passable. A Laïs takes up a man's silk hat that has been sat upon and crushed nearly flat, and wagers that she shall wear it in the Bois de Boulogne; the artist in chapeaux is summoned to her aid, and the unsightly thing, through the power of artful adjuncts, becomes a picturesque object; and the day following its exhibition a half dozen imitations show themselves on the *tour du lac*. The government places graceful groups in marble without the portals of the Grand Opera, and within fixes the form and the number of petticoats which each danseuse shall wear. It subsidizes art in its swaddling-clothes in the conservatories, and maintains it in its maturity in the same way in theatres and operas. The municipality of Paris constructs a capital which is a monument to art, the most beautiful in the world. The love of beautiful things is stimulated in every direction; its fruits are seen in every department of life; and it is plain that without such encouragement art would never have attained its present development. The authorities make the study of art a business, as they do the construction of bridges, the improvement of rivers and highways; and there is intelligent, educated direction in the expenditure of money for art purposes, the same as for practical objects. Our government may not go as far in this direction as that of France; but the art features of our capital attest that we might profit by what has been done in that artistic country, for much of the money that has been from time to time voted by Congress for art decoration has been simply thrown away.

CHAPTER 5

Words and Phrases

THE CHIEF characteristics of French are clearness, *finesse*, and precision. Its exactness admits of nothing vague, which is doubtless the reason why it has been so long employed as the language of diplomacy. For the expression of the wild, the horrible, the lofty, the terrible,—in a word, the tongue of genius, — English seems better. Such an opinion, however, is not accepted by Frenchmen, who naturally consider their tongue the most perfect of all. It is hard to judge the capacities of a foreign language with impartiality, because patriotism becomes involved in the question, to say nothing of the difficulty of understanding it as well as the native one. To know any one thing well is to exaggerate its merits; to the carpenter there is no instrument like the plane, and to the shoemaker there is nothing like leather. A few scientists of England have written their books in French; and one of these, Sir William Jones, the Orientalist, who apparently wrote with the same ease in both languages, held that French was the tongue of science, on account of its remarkable precision: but I do not recollect his making mention of any superior feature of his native language.

French is undoubtedly the language of conversation, in being chiefly composed of epigrammatic phrases and euphemisms, which seem to fit into every incident of social life. Peoples make their language to suit their character, and the French have naturally made theirs to this end. Our vehicle of thought would be too cumbrous for their airiness and vivacity. On the other hand, there is a richness in words, and a rugged boldness and strength, in the

English, which adapt it to the highest kind of eloquence, and the most stirring poetry. To the man born with the gift of bringing out its forces, it produces lasting effects that seem to be denied to the French. The utterances of Lacordaire, the modern Bossuet, were good for a day or a week; but those of one or two of his English or American contemporaries will be remembered by those who heard them, perhaps, as long as they live. Had Shakespeare been a complete master of French, and written his plays in the genius of that language, an Anglo-Saxon cannot help thinking that part of their power would be gone; that he would have failed in depth, grandeur, dignity, and that English humor of which his race is so fond; also in universality, for the French mind is not universal.

No one would think of denying to the French wonderful expression of a dramatic character. Their effects in speech are clear, well-defined, striking; and in their production the Frenchman is an artist unequalled. Our machinery of words is heavier, and more difficult to put in motion; but, when once set going by the man of genius, the results to us appear to be greater than can be effected through the French. The language of France is bristling with points almost ready made for the tongue; in English they must be made for use as they are required, and then, sharpened and burnished as they may be, are only blunt affairs. Gallic thrusts are light and rapid like the stroke of a rapier; those of the English are blunt and heavy as a club. The Frenchman has all his instruments for each particular purpose in his language, and kills a fly with a pin, and an ox with a spear, while we are apt to kill them both with the same weapon. One is light artillery, and the other heavy. One has the sharpness and delicacy of a Damascus blade; the other, the power of a bludgeon.

English being more a language of words than phrases, its forms are more varied, and it is more susceptible of originality. It allows, and indeed compels, individual choice; thus each one is forced in a measure to make a style of his own. Styles of French

writing naturally present differences, but not so great as in English. In the former hardly any extremes in a like number of French
contemporaries can be found equal to those exhibited in a group
of English writers, such as Hawthorne, Charles Reade, Ralph
Waldo Emerson, Edgar A. Poe, Charles Dickens, and Bret Harte,
each being distinctly and individually himself. A group of the
same number of the most widely differing writers of contemporary France would probably be composed of George Sand, Sainte-
Beuve, Victor Hugo, Alexandre Dumas père, Feydeau, and Paul
de Kock; a more diverging selection might be made of this nationality, as well as of English; but they are both approximative, and
the best occurring at this moment. To an impartial and competent
critic, the variety of style presented in the English is certainly
greater than that of the French group; one is composed of primary
colors, and the other of neutral tints, which in a great measure
is the result of the phrase feature. Given two-thirds of a phrase
in French, the critical reader can give a good guess as to the remaining words which complete it. The words are set into their
appropriate places in the sentence as mosaics are inserted to
make up a determinate whole. The logical sequences of the sentences themselves are almost as well known as the exact words
used for each occasion of life. Let the incident happen in a given
manner, and the conversation may almost be supplied in advance.
This represses originality of character in the style. Their method
in literary work, too, differs from ours. The chief aim with us
appears to be the delineation of character, as may be seen particularly in the works of Thackeray, where there is much good description of men and women, but remarkable absence of plot, and
consequently but little dramatic effect. This talent of personal
delineation was also the chief merit of Dickens. Charles Reade
may be regarded as an exception, for he makes plots, and works
them out according to the principles of art. When a Frenchman
does literary work, he seeks what he calls his mother idea which

pervades all, and on which all rests. This idea is never lost sight of; it is the *pourquoi* of every incident, and is the base on which is constructed what is called in technical language the *charpente*. Character delineation is always made subservient to scenical effects, and is sacrificed where it interferes with the active and regular development of the drama. Character receives its form and color chiefly from the action of the romance, while with us it is a portrait painted by the author. Thus the French are superior to the English in dramatic construction, but inferior in personal delineation.

With us language shapes itself from without and within. New words are created and old ones resuscitated at home, and contributions are levied on several modern tongues abroad. The language thus goes on changing and forming itself in entire freedom, according to the requirements and whims of the people. Foreign tongues exert but little or no influence on the French language, and whatever modifications and restrictions are placed on it come from within. There is a freedom in English in its government and progress which likens it to a democracy, while the submission of the French to the wishes of the French Academy brings it nearer to the tongue of an aristocracy. The French people seem to recognize the necessity of some such authority as the Academy to conserve the purity, order, and genius of their language, although they do not at all times acknowledge the wisdom of the dicta of that distinguished body. The Academy, for instance,—according to Paris journals, — does not admit the following words *décigramme, annexion, patroner, ausculter, désinvolture, détournement, discutable, illogique, insulter, progresser, prolétariat;* and it declares that *abbé, rabbin, sabbat,* and their derivatives only, double the *b;* according to which *gibbosité* would become *gibosité, gibbeux gibeux,* et cetera. There are critics who hold that the Academy, in its endeavor to inaugurate such a change of usage as that involved in the rejection of these words and the different spelling of others, has transcended its legitimate authority; and that it is hardly wise to allow elderly scholars out of the general movement of modern life, like those of the Academy, to shape the language which is always changing and moving onward to something better or worse; and that it would be better to have the privilege shared by younger men who are in the midst of the present and in a position to note the popular currents of speech.

There is such a love of administration in the French in every department of art and science, that they hardly get on without it in language; and so it is handed over to the Academy, where it is administered upon, like everything else in France. Were such a national institute founded on this side the water by act of Congress, — if such a thing were constitutional, — it would be safe to predict that its opinions would never be sanctioned as those of the French Academy are. The individual citizen here would be sure to exercise his own judgment in a matter of this kind, as he does in politics.

Whatever the influence of the venerable institution has been, there is an observable tendency within the last few years toward compactness in the French language; clearness it has always had. This tendency is as manifest in our own. One is soon satisfied of this in looking over the inflated July orations of the past, and the attenuated, interminable sentences of many of the early statesmen. Some of the elderly politicians of today still speak and write in this style. Emerson may be regarded, on this side, as a kind of John the Baptist of compact, concrete, virile writing. He of course did not create it, but he was one of the first to feel the power of such expression. A man of the old style would have beaten out one of his compact ten-paged essays into one of a hundred. The leading journals all bear evidence of this change in their cleverness and directness of statement. It has also modified conversation. Among novelists, the brief, vigorous sentences of Charles Reade have made him conspicuous in this kind of work. But a

Frenchman has gone further in this direction than our most advanced, — Hippolyte Taine. In most of his writing each small group of words—barely enough, and certainly not one too many — rapidly and graphically carries the idea to the reader; this quickly gives place to another, and so in succession, the whole showing that aversion to articles as parts of speech which characterizes our New England philosopher.

This trait of directness in writing is more general in all French literature than in ours, and is still more pronounced in speech. The subject may be of little interest, but the form is almost always good. As the French are a nation of talkers, much of what they say is not worth listening to, for it is impossible for those who are continually talking to be always talking well; but what is uttered is clear and idiomatic as far as each sentence goes. They talk for the sake of talking. At a table d'hôte or in a railway carriage, they have a knack, seldom possessed by an Englishman, of slipping easily, unrestrainedly, into conversation with their neighbors, though they have never seen them before. A glass of water, handing a newspaper, raising a window, passing a chair, lighting a cigar, and a hundred other things, are made the pretexts for opening up the way; and the conversation has not progressed five minutes before the beginner of it has insidiously slipped one or two compliments into the minds of those with whom he talks, to say nothing of that side-play in which he appears to attach importance to their opinions, and to listen to them with an occasional expression of approval. To most people the manner and speech of this man are very winning. Such a person meets an English traveller at table, who is doubtful about a sentence he has just pronounced to the Gaul, and says to his amiable companion apparently listening to him with much interest, that he is afraid that what he has said is hardly French; to which the Gallic convive answers, "No, monsieur, but it deserves to be." Impossible to be more polite. An instance is given of the opposite kind, showing the love of form in the last extremity: Malherbe is on his death-bed; to inspire him with fervor and resignation, his confessor describes the joys of Paradise, in which description he uses common and poorly constructed phrases. Having completed his description, he asks the dying man if he does not feel a great desire to enjoy these celestial pleasures. Malherbe answers, "Monsieur, speak of them no more; your wretched style has disgusted me with them."

Franklin left more sayings behind him than any of his countrymen, and prudence is the pivot on which they turn. But epigrammatic phrase is rarer in the mouths of our great men than those of France. Washington is credited with saying to Alexander Hamilton that he "almost waited for him," — an awkward translation of the words of Louis XIV. The "welcome with bloody hands to hospitable graves," of Corwin, is rather long and inflated. The "irrepressible conflict" of Seward is one of the best. It was the admonitory signal of national calamity, afterwards serving as a battle-flag. The "charity to all and malice toward none," of Lincoln, is good; besides, there was a certain twist in the phraseology of the late president which lent itself to epigram, — a twist difficult to describe, but easily recognized. The strength of his language is in striking contrast to the generally attenuated sentences of twenty or thirty years ago; and, as the tendency is now toward compactness, his speeches and papers will doubtless be more esteemed by posterity than they were by his contemporaries. However good the body of their speeches may have been, our great men have left scarcely any little groups of words that live. It is much the same with the British fathers: but few had the talent of sending a word quickly and directly to its exact destination, as a billiard player pockets a ball; and of these Sydney Smith was one of the most skilful, and not far behind him Horace Walpole, who in character was half a Frenchman. Every distinguished Frenchman has pronounced his memorable *mot,* — even to that humorous creation Joseph Prudhomme, with his, "Messieurs, ce sabre, c'est le plus beau jour de ma vie." One of the most quoted is that of Voltaire, with its alliterative jingle, "Canaux, canards, canaille," intended as a description of Holland. In popular estimation, a life, however noted, that does not furnish a mot, is regarded as incomplete.

It is interesting to note the change of signification in words common to English and French. *Susceptible,* as employed by us, usually means impressionable in matters of the heart, — easily won. The word which takes its place in French is *sensible:* thus when a person is susceptible, with them, he or she is sensible. When they use "susceptible" it has the significance of our "sensitive"; thus a person of a touchy, sensitive nature, is susceptible. Not infrequently the Englishman or American, in the general desire of saying something gallant to the French woman, tells her that he is susceptible, i.e., that he is a poor, sensitive kind of man, instead of the expansive, heart-in-hand sort of one he wishes to pass for. In *sensibility* we give the word its proper meaning, — the faculty of readily receiving impressions; but the adjective "sensible" commonly means practical, and is applied to one who has what is called good common sense. The French to express this quality often use *sensé* and *pratique,* but never *sensible;* and when the foreigner describes himself as — what he deems — a cool, practical, matter-of-fact man, he is really saying that he is a person of a susceptible nature, the reverse of what he means.

Again: *insensible* across the Channel means unconscious; a woman faints, and she is unconscious. On the other side, *insensible* is unfeeling, hard-hearted; there, when the woman faints, she loses *connaissance,* the faculty of knowing, and to describe the act the English have the advantage in brevity.

Anyone demented, with us, is crazy or insane; but when a man is raving mad he is a *maniac.* A much milder signification is given to the word in France. To be a maniac is generally nothing more than to be eccentric. A singular person is often described as one who has *des manies,* or who is *a maniaque.* It is even sometimes said of a person who is confirmed in his habits, *il est maniaque.*

To offer *excuses,* with us, is to furnish extenuating reasons for non-performance: to do so in France is to make an apology; but when the desire is to explain away at least part of the difficulty, and reinstate one's self in the estimation of the person offended, the meaning of our "excuse" is employed, but in another word, — *pardon.* I recollect once hearing an American suggest to a French woman to offer excuses to some one of his compatriots of her sex whom she had offended, when she quickly and rather tartly declined. Had he changed the word to "pardon," she would probably have acted on the suggestion. It may be said, however, that *excuse* as a substantive has also the same signification in French as in English; which is true, but it is so rarely used in social intercourse that practically such a sense can hardly be said to exist. As a rule, in ordinary conversation, each word has but one meaning; and whether lexicographers put this meaning as second or third, makes little difference to society, which knows no rule but its own. When the name "excuse" is turned into a verb, then it falls into the ranks with our English "excuse," and performs like service; returns, as it were, to its own, after dwelling in other households. Thus there is a considerable difference between the phrases, *Excusez-moi,* and *Je fais des excuses,* which requires no explanation to the Frenchman, so fully alive to any shade of meaning where his honor is concerned. When he makes excuses, he offers one of the humblest of apologies.

Accuser, to accuse, has a meaning used in correspondence unknown to us, namely, acknowledge; for instance, to accuse the reception of a letter. How it was pressed into such service is difficult to imagine. *Incessantly* with us is unintermitted continuance; *incessament*—the same word—with them is used for what is about to occur, and is nearly equivalent to our "presently."

Here, *actual* signifies the real; there, the present: as, MacMahon is *actuellement,* at present, the French president. *Actuality,* however, as a substantive, is beginning to make its appearance among us in the same sense as used by the French, —everyday, contemporary incident or circumstance, for which we have no exact word. The word is done to death in Gallic journalism, especially in that of an inferior kind, performing much the same work as the "situation," the "premises," "high-toned," and other words so much in vogue with partially-educated people among us.

There are differences between *gentleman* and *gentilhomme,* although one is often given as the translation of the other. "Gentleman" suggests a man of noble life—in England of noble birth —brave, generous, charitable, dignified, and in affluent circumstances. Some Britons are disposed to the belief that their island only rears this description of man; one of these, writing about France, said that even Guizot—one of the most intelligent— would never be able to understand and appreciate an English gentleman; a chauvinistic opinion that is naturally met with a smile on this side of the Atlantic, and a shrug across the Channel. *Gentilhomme* brings to the mind the courtier of Louis XV. and of the Regency, of touchy honor, possessed of tact, elegance, and *finesse,* rich, prodigal, and full of gallantry; a maker of madrigals and *mots.* The word does not seem to fit the modern man who has taken the place of the ancient. *Gentilhomme* belongs to the powdered hair, the sword, and the knee-breeches of the past, and adapts itself with a poor grace to the contemporary surrounded by steam, telegraph, and modern politics. Some French writers, recognizing this change, now actually employ the English word in preference.

The word *fine* usually has another meaning than that given to it in English. A fine woman, for instance, with us, is a well-looking or an amiable person: a fine woman of France is full of tact and cleverness, with a shade of irony and want of confidence. The determination to succeed is also a part of "fine," and thus fortified it is a strong word and often employed. As an illustration of tongue *finesse:* Napoleon tries to get a book from a shelf above his head, but cannot reach it, when an aide-de-camp, stepping forward, says, "Sire, permit me to reach it: I am higher than you."

" You are longer," is the correction from Bonaparte the *fin.*

Again: "Si la République abolit la guillotine, on pourra dire d'elle, la République est le gouvernement qui divise le moins."

In English *transpire* means to become known; in French, to *perspire,* which seems to be its correct derivative signification. In the substantive *figure,* both languages started from the same point, form, and then diverged. In the ordinary language of social commerce, when the English *figure* is pronounced, the general form of the body is always understood, and especially that of the woman, she being more naturally given to outlines and ornaments than man; in French the face is meant. More work is had out of the verb there than here; one of the Gaul's favorite fashions of beginning a narrative or an anecdote being, "Figurez-vous, mon cher." The substantive has yielded a derivative or two more on the other side than here; one of them, *figurante,* however, is being incorporated into our tongue since the advent of opera bouffe.

The word *desolation* brings before the Anglo-Saxon a picture of sore affliction, — a tempest passing over the soul, and leaving it a wreck abandoned of God and man, a grand isolated grief; and, having contemplated such a tableau, he finds, on turning to his Gallic neighbors, that they are in the habit of conjuring up such a scene every quarter of an hour to convey an idea of their regrets at not meeting an acquaintance, or at not reaching quick enough to pick up a woman's glove before she performs that office herself.

Confound pictures to the imagination a stroke of misfortune, — Babel smitten with a hundred tongues, the waters of the Red Sea closing around King Pharaoh, the dagger of Brutus before the eyes of Caesar, or any other great and sudden catastrophe. In French, the word generally performs a more gentle and pleasing office: the man says to the woman who hands him a flower, a book, or a cup of tea, "Madame, votre bonté me confond." Their word, in short, to ours, is as a flute to a bugle.

When at theatres or soirées, with their necessity of expansion, they identify themselves more than we do with those furnishing the entertainment. By applause and compliments they show apparently that they have as much at heart the success of the evening as the hostess or the actors; in a word, they take a part in it; hence they *assist* at a representation or a ball where we are only present.

In English, when *character* is spoken of, it means reputation; in French, disposition or temper, as such a one has a *bon* or *mauvais caractère*. In another sense, where we call an eccentric man a *character,* they say he is an *original.*

We have no affectionate term for our country, and the nearest English approach to it is comprised in the words Old England. The Germans have Vaterland, but the French have something better, —*patrie.* There is a meaning and an attraction in this word to the French people which those who have not lived among them can hardly understand. The exile, the soldier, and the colonist pronounce it with a passionate ardor unknown to the Anglo-Saxon tongue, and legions have died with it on their lips. It breathes the spirit of tenderness and affection, and is one of the most sacred words of the language. On the other hand, if we have not their endearing word for country, we possess one for our dwelling-place of which their language is destitute, — *home. A* few of their writers use it, but sparingly, and as a foreign word. Had they been less circumscribed in their ideas in this respect, it would long since have been a part of their speech, especially as its pronunciation offers no difficulty to the French tongue. What they *have* taken from us are not the words most required, and are generally corrupted, like *rosbif* for roast beef, *dogue-car* for dog-cart, *bifteck* for beefsteak, *pouding* for pudding, &c.

In English vernacularism, when the woman has tender inclinations toward the man, she calls him her *beau;* but why thus called, especially when he is ugly, would doubtless be difficult for her to explain. An effort to mend this matter is occasionally made by substituting "sweetheart"; but it does not exactly answer, owing to the feminine character usually implied in the word. As the French have more men given to paying court to women than we, there is a fuller nomenclature, although the admirer as "beautiful" does not figure therein. The glove-girl calls the one persistent buyer who frequents her establishment with gallant intentions, her monsieur. If it be subsequently discovered that it is for the *bon motif,* he becomes her *prétendant.* In the lower strata of blouse folk, the admirer is simply described as *mon homme.* The grisette permits herself a greater range in speaking of him who avows himself her slave, as well as of the feelings he inspires. She has a *toquade* for him; *il lui tape dans l'oeil; elle est folle de lui,* and other phrases more expressive than elegant. All classes recognize at least four conditions of the heart in the intercourse of man and woman, described in *la grande passion, l'amour, l'amourette,* and *la galanterie,* to which has recently been added our *flirtation,* — one of the very few English words, according to French opinion, worthy of being taken into the language.

Coup de lapin, "stroke of the rabbit," is one of those eccentricities of speech not apt to be heard in the drawing-room, although its fair occupants understand but too well what it means. The woman in France generally conserves her freshness up to forty or forty-five; and when she reaches the critical point where she begins to lose it, — in a word, when she begins to decline, — she receives a stroke of the rabbit. The subject has been treated with pencil: a somewhat mature woman is portrayed in evening costume with something melancholy in her face, while a rabbit sits on his haunches behind on the back of her chair; his ears are pricked, and his eyes are intently fixed on the woman; one of his paws is raised, with which he is about to administer the direful tap on the back of her nude neck. To the French woman, who as a rule is coquettish, this is the most dreadful stroke which can befall her.

Epanchement de famille is a phrase which slips smoothly from the French tongue; but its translation comes somewhat awkwardly from that of the Anglo-Saxon, probably because he has so little of the trait thus described.

In the home of the phrase, effusion and familiarity extend to all members of the family. A son of eighteen or twenty playfully pulls the paternal whiskers, and the act involves no loss of fatherly dignity; he makes a confidante of his mother, and tells her the details of his love affairs, such as an Englishman would never speak of to his most intimate male companion. Madame de Sévigné, still a reigning model of good taste, invited her son to these confidences, which she afterwards communicated to her daughter, clothed in the delicate periphrase that she knew so well how to weave around the questionable incidents of life. The majority of her countrywomen of today follow her example in trying to initiate themselves into the peccadilloes of their beloved Jules and Oscars. Their relations with their daughters are of the most intimate character; they have scarcely a thought that is not shared in common, and this communion is marked by half a dozen tender embraces during the day. These familiar acts are naturally accompanied with language of a like complexion; and for this purpose they have remarkable help of which we are destitute, — the *tutoiement*. We are obliged to confuse friends with acquaintances and strangers in the *you,* and are unable to define the limits of an intimate circle. French children grow up under the sunshine of *tu* and *toi,* and it undoubtedly has a happy influence on their lives. So many affectionate caresses would have been incomplete without the word to express them, and *tutoiement* is that faithful interpreter.

Je suis Français is a phrase often heard in France. If an imputation be made on a man's courage, his figure is drawn up to its greatest altitude, and the words are uttered as if from Olympian heights. If he takes what he deems a noble stand worthy of himself and his country, he taps himself on the breast, and the three words follow. If a reflection be made on that honor about which there is so much talk, the phrase of three words is pronounced with an intimation that excuses must be offered with the alternative of blood-letting. Rudely crowd a man at the theatre or the railway station, and two to one he will say, "Don't push me, sir: I am a Frenchman"; implying that you may possibly do so to others with impunity, but not to a man of his nationality.

One sees in the Anglo-Saxon a disposition to jest at death, as in the gibes of the grave-diggers before Hamlet, and the Western journal which said its State was so healthy that in order to start a graveyard the citizens had to borrow a corpse from a neighboring State. This effort to encircle a death's-head with a garland of humor shocks the Gaul. *La mort* is not used in a jocular vein. With us young people not unfrequently go to the cemeteries to amuse themselves: this would strike him as singular. He respectfully removes his hat as he meets a funeral procession, and as he passes before the house of death. Tombstone wit is rare, and Boileau showed a disregard of public opinion when he penned such an epigram as this:

> "Ci-gît ma femme. Ah, qu'elle est bien
> Pour son repos et le mien!"

When one of his fellows is keen-sighted, the Gaul says he has the American eye, which probably has its origin in his acquaintance with the works of Cooper; for, if he be ignorant of every other American author, he always knows this one. When he says he is sick at the heart, this is one of his graceful evasions, and he means that he is sick at the stomach. When he speaks of a man as sober, he refers to his temperament, and it has no connection in his mind with the absence of drunkenness. Our windows look, and his give, on the street. The American imbecile will never set the river on fire; the French one has not invented powder. Romeo waiting at the rendezvous for his Juliet, he calls the hour of the shepherd. We call a spade a spade, and he calls a cat a cat. When the time for paying comes, with nothing in the purse, he describes it as the ugly quarter of an hour of Rabelais. In America a stupid man is a goose: in France he is a turkey. The French duck we have acclimated, and it bears on its back the burden of our shams and false reports.

Anglo-Saxons are apt to take for granted that they enjoy a monopoly of *humor,* that they only have the thing as well as the name; but it is an ancient French word, and was employed in the English sense by Corneille, in whose plays it is found. Then it fell into desuetude, and was revived by Diderot. Of the late writers, Sainte-Beuve gives one of the best English applications of the word, where he says, in speaking of Chateaubriand, that he had a kind of humor, or fantasy, *qui se joue sur un fond triste,* — a description, by the way, that would apply equally well to the character of President Lincoln. Humor in the English sense is specific; in the French it is almost a synonyme of caprice, leaving aside its primary signification. The French possess this quality in common with us, but with the condition that mirth shall not master art; there must be no coarseness in the exhibition. The Gaul cannot see the amusement of a man with a hat knocked over his eyes; he does not laugh when another falls, however awkwardly he may sprawl. The distortion of language in the search after droll effects does not move him to mirth. Though he understood our language as well as ourselves, he would never learn to be amused with the deformed orthography of some of our humorists; these broken-backed words and twists of language would only offend his taste.

He who has read Molière, and frequented the Palais Royal theatre, readily concedes humor to the nation, but it is difficult to seize its conception of it. When a copy of "Punch" is submitted to the Gaul, he smiles out of politeness; his eye does not brighten with pleasure over the follies of Rotten Row or the mishaps of hunters going over fences and ditches; but there is a change of expression when he catches sight of "Charivari," with the comicalities of Cham and his confrères. Then he is at home, and his gayety expands. Here are specimens at random, in accordance with his idea of the humorous: —

Phryné loses her child. "The little cherub is in heaven," observes a sympathizing friend by way of consolation. "That is what distresses me: I am sure of never seeing him again," returns the weeping mother.

A man in blouse, in the Belleville Quarter, presents a bottle of perfume to his beloved, saying, "When you smell that you will regret that your Creator did not make you all nose."

This is headed "La Propagande:" the heart of an opulent woman of forty is ardently besieged by a man of fifty, in spectacles, and on his knees, whom she resists, saying, "Non, Oscar, pas tant qu'il y aura des Prussiens sur notre sol." Another shows a grandmother with an infant in her arms, to which she gives the bottle, the former bearing the well-known traits of Thiers, the latter being the republic in its swaddling-clothes.

With us the man of culture is more easily discovered from his speech. With them there are many current phrases common to several classes, and there are shopmen who pronounce them nearly as well as the people of culture. When to the employment of these phrases is added a smartness of dress and manner, — say in the *coiffeur* and the *valet de chambre*, — a certain sameness seems to envelop all. This is the case in the matter of speech; but wealth and education are more generally manifested in other ways with them than with us, such as general bearing and surroundings, Legion of Honor, and speech when the line of platitudes is passed. With us a man with a three-days' beard, a mouth full of tobacco, and a felt hat, may possess wealth and official position. This would be a striking incongruity in France. The imitative faculty is much developed in the Gaul; and the valet seizes his master's manner and speech as no Englishman in the same station of life could ever do. This, naturally, as long as he keeps near shore in current vocabulary; but, when he goes beyond, the resemblance deepens into caricature.

Word decoration is hung about everything, and ordinary and sometimes mean things have fine names. An eight-by-ten room is a *salon;* a lobster is the cardinal of the sea — presumably after being boiled; stewed mutton is *mouton à la paysanne;* a hairdresser is an *artiste;* an editor is *redacteur-en-chef;* the letter-writer closes his epistle with a string of magnificent words. The Gaul is always putting his best foot foremost. To have a decoration of the Legion of Honor, and not wear it, would imbitter his life. If he has ever held any position related to the government, however remotely, he ever afterward inscribes it below his name on cards and letters; and one not unfrequently sees printed on the cards of provincials, "Ancien capitaine des pompiers," "Ancien membre du conseil municipal," &c., which are grotesquely pompous.

In the drawing-room of France there is a marked disposition for general conversation, where each one places his word à propos, and passes the subject back to his neighbors; thus all contribute their quota. The wit of the salon is exacting as to tone and delicacy, and yet it may be everything in this respect without being rigorous or thorough. Certain modes of banal expression are discordant, the same as certain acts: for instance, no one would dream of passing first through a doorway; of helping one's self at the table, and passing the dish; of speaking only with one of two persons who are present, because that one happens to be the most agreeable. There are those finical enough to consider "Comment vous portez-vous?" addressed to a woman as coarse; for which they substitute, "Oserais-je m'informer de la santé de madame?" Such a one is careful to ask for "du vin de Champagne," but never "du champagne." Words and actions of the lightest shade of disagreeability are avoided with much tact. "On badine au salon, on blague dans l'atelier." This, for instance, is the wit of the workshop:

"Oh, madame! —le joli bébé. Il est à vous?"

"Oui, monsieur, c'est mon *dernier.*"

"Oh, ce serait dommage."

And this of the drawing-room: —

"The pure legitimists write *roy* for *roi.* The Y, say they, is an I which majestically raises its two hands to heaven. Oh, heaven pardon them! they know not what they say."

There is something of the stoic, real or affected, with us, which keeps back speech. To talk seems to be an acquired talent to the Anglo-Saxon, and a natural gift to the Frenchman. The men of few words in England and America form a large class; and in the former, especially, the silent man is esteemed. Yet these men of niggard speech can express themselves when roused to it, as they occasionally prove by speaking before public meetings. This talent, so common in America, is rare in France. It is a pleasure to the Gaul to stand beside a mantlepiece, and communicate his thoughts in colloquial form to six or eight men and women, or, seated at table, to send them over the crystal and flowers to other convives not exceeding a dozen; but to stand up before a public audience is a possible disaster that he will not confront. When one thinks, as a rule, how easily he is abashed before an audience, his ease and aplomb before a drawing-room group appear remarkable. He has rapidity of thought and an Irishman's fluency, but to make a sustained effort before a body of people is beyond the ordinary type. The redundancy of words in the English admits of a certain vagueness which possibly renders public speaking easier. Cromwell is cited as one who could talk half an hour without saying anything, and yet no Englishman could be more direct than he when he desired.

The epigram naturally finds development in the dialect of the boulevards, otherwise known as the *langue verte*. It is here where new words first appear; that is, generally, old words with a new signification. It is seldom, for instance, that a word is created like *pignouf;* and the etymologists, in their desire to provide all words with a regular derivation, hardly admit that even this is a creation. *Pignouf,* like our *skedaddle,* has no legitimate father and mother; it is a child of the people. The eccentricities of the *langue verte* are often heard on the boulevards, and some of them are easily recalled. A tall, thin woman is an *asperge montée.* A man whose reason is somewhat impaired has a spider in his ceiling (head). A brave fellow, *quel lapin!* Whatever is very handsome is *truffé de galbe.* The milk in the cocoanut is the *truc.* A woman who has abandoned the straight path has *cascadé.* To attack with energy is to *lâcher tout.* To feel the influence of wine is to be *allumé.* To lose money is to be *lavé.* The exclamation which blasts frail legs with ridicule is *quelles flûtes!* To restore circulation to one's legs by dancing is to *asticoter ses flûtes.* The discovery of a snare is hailed with *balançoire* or *carotte.* Scepticism is denoted by the question, *Et ta soeur?* Swells are designated as *des gens pourris de chic.* Splendid is *épatant.* To be taken in, or done, *mis dedans,* or *frit. Zût!* cuts off all further parley. He who has taken too much wine belongs to the *paroisse de Saint-Jean-le-Rond.* He who asks, *As-tu fini?* means that dust cannot be thrown in his eyes. To be a wallflower is to figure as tapestry.

A little of this slang is heard in the drawing room from the mouths of very fashionable women. It is a gift of the Gallic horsemen who have appeared these latter days like an irruption in

Paris and its neighborhood, and shows that man makes woman now, as he did in the Garden of Eden. But French women generally do not have recourse to slang to show their wit. They usually follow in the traditions of their elders, and attach more importance to style than eccentricity; and, if their sallies are not as brilliant now as in the old salon days, it is because men do not have as much time to listen to them. Nor do men now say things under the chandelier with the smartness of the eighteenth century. There is still power in the uttered epigram of today, but it does not remove ministers nor unsettle governments. What was then sped from the lips of courtiers is now launched through the columns of a journal. The ammunition of the gentleman of the palace has passed into the hands of the editor; and one of Voltaire's phrases pointed with satire was then what a broadside from a leading journal is now.

CHAPTER 6

The Poor

THERE IS A BRANCH of the French Government for relieving the
necessities of the suffering poor, which is under the control of the
minister of the interior, and is called the Assistance Publique.
Under the law creating this bureau, assistance was obligatory,
that is, the poor man had a right to demand charity of the State;
but, as this was followed by abuses and frauds, the law has been
so modified as to allow the Government discretionary power in
dispensing charity, except in the cases of foundlings *(enfants
trouvés)* and the insane poor. Under the present system, prudence
is combined with humanity. With the administrative centraliza-
tion which exists in France, the minister of the interior directs
public charities over all points of the country. He also exercises
immediate control over certain establishments, such as the asylum
for the insane of Charenton, the institutions of the deaf and dumb
and blind children, and the hospice of the Quinze-Vingts. He also
aids a great number of private establishments of charity with
subsidies from the state, and in certain cases is allowed to grant
personal relief.

To reach the sensitive poor who have not the temerity to demand public assistance, the Government has an organization for
the distribution of alms in the domiciles of the needy. It is considered in the interests of society and the poor themselves to encour-
age this feeling; for it is, found, that, when there is no hesitation
in claiming public aid, it is accompanied with a certain demoral-
ization which is difficult to cure. Hence, when the authorities give
alms, they do so as privately as they can. There is a small bureau

in each *arrondissement* of Paris, controlled by each mayor, who acts under the instruction of the prefect of the Seine, who in turn is under the orders of the minister of the interior. The prefect of the Seine is the president of a council of public assistance, which is occupied with the practical working and carrying out of all public plans of charity. The ramifications of this branch of administration are extensive, and reach all cases of misfortune and destitution from the cradle to the grave: the servants of this bureau always perform their duties with a due regard to the dignity of the poor. One of the small organizations within the grand one is that for the resuscitation of the drowned; and a case came under my own observation which attested its efficiency.

It occurred one morning as I was crossing over to the Latin Quarter by the Pont Neuf, and had reached that part of the bridge where the equestrian statue of Henri IV. stands. I observed a group of men pulling a man out of the water, apparently drowned. I knew that the authorities had a special service of soldiers for the rescue of the drowned; and I was curious to see the means employed for resuscitation, and drew near to the scene. It was easy to see that the group of men in uniform were trained to the work, for they proceeded with order and activity, but without precipitation. As soon as the man was drawn out of the water, he was laid on his right side, the face turned toward the ground, and the jaws gently opened to facilitate the escape of water, of which there is much less than is popularly believed in such cases. Several times the head was placed a little lower than the body, for the same purpose, but only allowed to remain in this position a few seconds. This process was alternated with another,—the manipulation to induce breathing, which consisted in pressing the abdomen, stomach, and sides of the chest, but softly. These efforts were without effect: the man looked as if he had seen the last of earth. Only a few moments were taken up with these preliminary trials; then the prostrate figure was carried quickly to the nearest station on the banks of the Seine for the rescue of the drowned, called the bureau of the "Secours aux Noyés," whither I followed. The carrying and handling were done without jolting or roughness, the head being held higher than the body. On arriving at the station, the man was stripped and wiped dry, a flannel cap was placed on his head, and he was laid between two blankets on a straw mattress. The process of laying on the side was here resumed, and the mouth was cleansed with the fingers of one of the operators. The manipulation to induce respiration was also resumed, with intervals of about a quarter of a minute between each pressure, which was repeated fifteen or twenty times: this was followed by a suspension of ten minutes.

While the operation was going on, remarks were made in the group such as, "Pauvre diable! il a cassé sa pipe;" "Il n'aura plus mal aux dents!" showing that they were not hopeful of the result. Perhaps twenty minutes had elapsed after the arrival at the station when the physician employed on this service made his appearance, and took direction of the case. A piece of soft wood was introduced between the teeth to keep the mouth open. A warming-pan filled with hot water was passed over the body on the outside of the blanket, down the spinal column as well as along the front of the body. The pit of the stomach and the sides of the chest just under the arms were especially subjected to this treatment. This was alternated with a gentle friction of hot woollen mittens and the naked hands, when, the soles of the feet and palms of the hands were much rubbed in addition to other portions of the body. An operator breathed into the mouth of the man by means of a tube. Once or twice, while this was going on, the physician consulted a thermometer, to see that the temperature of the chamber was at the requisite degree. The efforts so far proving in vain, the doctor had recourse to the fumigating process, which consists in the introduction of tobacco smoke into the intestines. When this had proceeded about ten minutes the man gave a feeble sign of life, at which there were ejaculations of satisfaction. When the occupant of the mattress made an effort to breathe, all manipulation was discontinued, lest it should interfere with the natural movement. Almost imperceptibly the chest rose and fell, and in the effort there were indications of a desire to vomit, which was encouraged by introducing a feather into the throat. After the vomiting, the breathing came slowly, the bed and blankets were warmed with the warming-pan, and the patient was left in repose, when he went to sleep.

The physician, on learning the name of him who had discovered the drowning man and hauled him ashore, said to him, "Well, Jacques, you have earned your twenty-five francs," this being the sum that is given by the authorities when the person is resuscitated.

From a scrap of paper in the pocket, the identity of the person was discovered, as well as the motive of the attempt at self-destruction. He was a *chiffonnier* of the name of Pierre, and he wanted to drown himself because Justine had jilted him for Jean.

A few days after, I went into the street which was the scene of Pierre's unfortunate love experience. It was a narrow, twisting, sombre lane behind the Pantheon, beyond the Latin Quarter, — the heart of the quarter of the chiffonniers. This thoroughfare is about nine feet wide, with narrow pavements on each side not exceeding two feet in width. There is a general odor of the kitchen, in which the onion predominates. All along people are lounging and gossiping in the middle of the lane, or leaning against the houses. Through the windows of the drinking shops are seen groups playing cards or dominoes on dark little wooden tables, and stout women serving behind zinc-covered counters, and joking with the consumers. The houses are tall and gloomy, the lights being confined to the ground floors. An unusual number of policemen are observed, which is a pretty sure indication of the turbulence of the population. Near the lower end of the lane, the groups are more numerous under a great lamp on which is painted in red letters the word *Bal*. At the end of a long passage, a man is seated behind a rack, who receives the entrance money for the ball, — five sous. Sticks and umbrellas must be deposited with him — a precautionary measure — at an extra charge of two sous, for which he gives a dirty pasteboard check. A few steps farther on is a large, low, long room, on one side of which, on an elevated place, their heads close to the ceiling, are six or eight very ordinary musicians, who play with much vigor. A low railing surrounds the space allotted for dancing, and on the outside of the railing are small tables and wooden benches, most of which are occupied by men in blouse and cap, women, and children. Most of the men are smoking clay pipes, and here and there a woman is smoking a cigarette. The tables are garnished with wine-bottles and glasses, and great zinc bowls in which is made wine-punch, the favorite beverage of the establishment.

A half-dozen policemen are stationed in different parts of the room, and their uniform in this place is a pleasant thing for the eye of the visitor to dwell upon. Within the railing the dancing proceeds with energy, the charge being two sous for each dance for each couple, the man naturally defraying the expense. There are instances, however, where the woman, tired of her rôle as a wallflower, furnishes the money to some needy cavalier. The person who receives the two sous is a man of authority, who stands near the centre of the ball-room floor, inviting all in a loud voice to come forward and participate in the Terpsichorean entertainment. At this, an irreverent thought enters my mind of the revivalist preacher calling upon the brethren and sisters to come forward to the mourner's bench. "Avancez, avancez, messieurs et mesdames, on va commencer," cries this man. "Ça va être *rigolo* —une musique *ébouriffante;* avancez!" When the dancing is under way, whether waltz or quadrille, the music stops, and the dance-stimulator collects the two sous from each couple; which rather indicates a want of confidence in the solvency of the dancers.

There is no exhibition of grotesque gesture, eccentric step, nor lofty leg-lifting. There are no "artists" here, but people whose limbs have lost their litheness through labor. There is rather more activity among the women than the men, the former jumping about with considerable energy, but little grace. It can hardly be expected that he who bends for several hours under a basket of rags, in his nightly rounds, should display much grace. He shuffles and jumps to the measure, and this suffices. In the waltz, he clasps his partner closely with both arms, and whirls away to the very last strain.

Naturally there is much slang in the vocabulary of these poor votaries of pleasure, and some of it is grotesque. I overheard a man inviting a woman to dance with the words, "Madame, voulez-vous *gigotter* avec moi?" another, "Madame, voulez-vous vous *asticoter* les jambes un peu?" — and this with indescribable gesture.

In the intervals of music, there is a buzz of gossip and laugh along the tables, where the people look at the dancers, and make comments on them. Then follows the squeaking and sawing music, and then the "Avancez, messieurs et mesdames," &c.; and so on to the end.

The face of one of the gayest and most vigorous dancers seems familiar to me. He clasps a young woman in his arms, and is whirling around to one of Hervé's waltzes as I examine him, and try to fix him in my memory. It is Pierre, the man who, a few days previously, wanted to die. I learn from the policeman near me that it is Justine with whom he is waltzing; that the proof of his affection in throwing himself into the Seine for her brought her back to him, with which the dramatic feature of the act, and the consequent notoriety, had something to do.

A little old man in blouse and felt hat, at one of the tables, is pointed out to me by the policeman as one, who, in addition to rag-picking, deals in questionable rabbits. He is known as the Père Jacques, and is regarded as a person of some importance in the rag fraternity. I approach Père Jacques, and engage him in conversation. He has become expansive over his wine, and makes indiscreet revelations touching the rabbit business. Twenty years ago he skinned and dressed his rabbits, and people bought them without asking any questions. That was the *bon temps;* and, if it had continued, he would be today a man of independent fortune. But the journals and inquisitive people got to talking so much about cats in connection with rabbits, that a long season of dulness followed as a consequence. The newspapers went so far as to figure up how many rabbits were brought into Paris each year, and how many were consumed; and they made it out that twice as many were consumed as were brought in. He felt for a time as if the business was ruined; for, thereafter, the rabbit purchasers demanded the head of the rabbit as a guaranty of the genuineness of the animal. But he was equal to the emergency. He gave an extension to his commerce by making an arrangement with all the cooks on his rag-beat to buy their rabbit-skins, on condition that the heads should be delivered with them. Thereafter he was enabled to furnish to sceptical buyers the rabbit head with the dressed cat, and everybody was satisfied. He sold the animals to the small out-of-the way restaurants, as a rule, where they were made into *gibelottes.* The cat entire yielded him one franc; and they to whom he sold the flesh usually got about two and a half francs out of the animal when turned into *gibelottes.* The business was fair; but there was more competition, especially since the Commune, under which some people had learned to eat the cat with pleasure, knowing him to be cat.

It is hardly necessary to add that the Père Jacques was obliged to conduct his business with mystery, in view of provisions contained in the municipal regulations against the sale of certain kinds of meat, especially those employed in the manufacture of sausages, Italian cheese, and pot-pies, all of which are comprised in the general word *charcuterie*. Considering the vigilance exercised by the authorities over the preparation of such aliments, one can infer that the Père Jacques was obliged to observe much discretion in the disposal of his feline flesh. It was to the interest of buyer and seller to keep the commerce secret; and, so far, the père had escaped detection. M. Jacques thought it was an injustice, that, under the republic, a man could not eat cat-meat if he wanted to, and he solemnly protested against such tyranny.

He is in a loquacious mood; and, among other things, he informs me that he has a friend who has a specialty in the way of cocks' combs. There are a number of amateurs of a dish composed of this head-gear; and his friend met the increasing demand by making an artificial article out of beef tongues, which was so skilfully done, that experienced cooks could not tell the difference. His friend even insisted that he improved upon nature; that there were irregularities and faults in most of the combs of cocks, which he ameliorated through art. His friend is also of the fraternity of ragpickers, as, indeed, are almost all who are present. As I quit the place, Père Jacques calls for another punch. Pierre is at one of the tables, with his arm around the waist of Justine; the music saws away, and the man in the centre of the floor continues to cry out, "Avancez, messieurs et mesdames," &c.

The ragpicker is attached to his calling from the liberty which he fancies it gives him. Under his rags, this Diogenes has his pride, and considers himself superior to a domestic. He sleeps, eats, and drinks in freedom: if he gets sick, the hospital is ready to receive him. Thus he lives in ignorance, dirt, and laziness until gathered to his fathers. The chiffonniers are divided into two classes, — the diurnal and nocturnal. The latter begin their peregrinations as soon as the public sweepers have left the streets. The most desirable quarters are those of the rich, such as the Faubourg Saint-Germain, Saint-Honoré, and the streets in the neighborhood of the Triumphal Arch. They usually become known to the cooks of their respective rounds, and often receive from them sufficient remains of food for their sustenance. When this is the case, there is an understanding, tacit or expressed, that the chiffonnier shall restore any object of value which he may find in the débris. Besides the pleasures of the ball and the wine-shop, the chiffonnier sometimes allows himself the amusement furnished in one of the small theatres of the Barrier, where the play is usually a melodrama of sanguinary character, in which the villain is invariably punished in the last act. In regard to this last feature, the ragpicker is an exacting critic.

As a rule, the ragpicker does not possess any furniture of his own, but lives in hired lodgings, and for the time being. He pays four sous in advance for a bed of loose straw, on which he throws himself without doffing his sorry garments. There are long, gloomy chambers where the lodgers sleep in common, for two sous, and where the Amphytrion, in case of nocturnal disturbance, appears with a club, and restores peace. The ragpicker speaks the *argot* known to thieves and social outcasts, but this is not the same argot which is employed on the Boulevards, as some people are inclined to believe. One is not without certain pretensions to elegance and wit; the other is vulgar and often brutal. In the argot of the chiffonnier, the tongue is called *menteuse;* love, *dardant;* and a book, *babillard.* Everything which he considers beautiful, or which excites his admiration, is *rupin* or *chenu.* His phrase for punishment, *l'abbaye de Mont-à-Regret,* is not without humor.

To work as little as possible, and drink much, is the chiffonnier's idea of happiness. To lie at length on the ground, and bask in the sun, is also one of the most desirable features in his programme. In his disputes, epithets are bandied about with alacrity, accompanied with energetic gesture. If they warm to the fighting point, according to an old tradition still observed, they pull off their shirts, point to their naked shoulders, and cry out to each other as they do so, "Look at that: it has never been marked. Can you say as much?" This insult is usually followed by an act; they clinch, and have it out. They like disorder, and possess a lively inclination for a *rixe;* hence are always ready for a revolution. This principally arises from their having nothing to lose in the fall of governments, or the reign of anarchy, and perhaps something to gain. During the Commune, some of them were prominent persons.

The chiffonnier conveys the contents of his basket to a merchant who buys and assorts what is brought to him. The assorting of this débris is another trade, which is called *trillage,* in which men and women are employed, who are named *trilleurs.* They pass twelve hours a day at this kind of work in the midst of the most unhealthy exhalations.

It may not be an uninteresting fact to those who eat *croûte au pot* soup in Paris, to know that in some of the restaurants the little roasted pieces of bread which they like in their soup often come from the basket of the chiffonnier. This is more especially the case with the small roasted crumbs which are put into soups known as *purées aux croûtons.* The only thing that can be said in extenuation is, that these scraps of bread have been roasted, and it is an axiom of the kitchen that fire purifies everything.

There is a certain kind of organization among the chiffoniers by which each one has his separate quarter in the pursuit of his calling. Those who have good quarters derive a reasonable compensation for their labor; but those who are condemned to poor ones obtain but a miserable pittance, and with them the material life is reduced to its minimum proportions. The following is a list of the expenses of one of the poorest per diem:

	Sous.
An *arlequin* (mixture of meat, vegetables, and other ingredients, — "crumbs from the rich man's table")	2
A glass of violet-colored liquid called wine	2
A pound of bread, odd pieces	2
	—
Comprising the breakfast	6
Dinner the same	6
A bed of straw in company with others	2
	—
Total	14

The word "ragpicker"does not cover the range of operations; for the ragpickers take up bones, pieces of glass, skins of animals, rags of linen, wool, and cotton, bits of food, shreds and scraps of luxury, and, in short, all the débris of civilization. In their *argot* the woman calls the great willow basket which she bears on her back her *willow cashmere,* and the man calls it his *cabriolet.* With the pendent lamp on the end of a piece of straight wire reaching almost to the ground in one hand, and the iron rod hooked at the end in the other, and the basket on his back, the chiffonnier is equipped. In this harness he silently follows the gutters of the streets, near which are thrown the little piles of refuse, turns them up quickly with the hook, and conveys whatever there is of any value, with a dexterous movement, into his basket. In these nocturnal peregrinations he is wholly intent on his business, looking neither to the right nor the left.

According to the last census returns there are one hundred and fourteen café-concerts in Paris, in which the "artists" receive from three to five francs an evening. A number of these establishments are situated in the poor quarters, and furnish almost the only amusement within the reach of the blouse people.

One of the strangest and least known of these is the Concert des Oiseaux in the Ménilmontant Quarter, near the cemetery of Père Lachaise. It is not thus named, as one might suppose, because birds sing there, but because it is situated in the street of the Concert des Oiseaux, which is a narrow, tortuous way, entangled in a network of like ways or alleys, rather difficult to find. Sad, sombre, old-fashioned houses, or dilapidated walls, are its principal characteristics. The concert takes place in an old brick house, over the entrance of which is the sign, "Concert varié trois fois par semaine." The concert-room is attached to a wine-shop, which has the sign over its door of "Souvenir de Béranger." Close to the sign is a portrait of the national songster, or, rather, a caricature. There is another sign in large letters, namely, "Ici on fait sa cuisine soi-même." In the inside there is a large furnace which is fired twice a day, where the poor, men, women, and children, come and cook their provisions. Much of what they bring is the refuse of the rich man's table, or of an inferior quality, whether of meat or vegetables. The master of the place furnishes the gridiron, the stewpan, and the fire, and charges only one sou on each dish. His profit is rather on the wine, which they buy from him from eight to ten sous the litre, and which they drink with their repasts. It is against the rules for a client to bring his own wine. In the evening, after the repast, the diners may pass from the eating-room — which is also the kitchen — into the concert-room.

There are other concerts of this kind in the Grenelle and Charonne Quarters, and in Mouffetard Street, the latter being much frequented by the chiffonniers. In one of these the beer costs only five sous and the coffee three, the purchase of either entitling the consumer to all the privileges of the establishment.

In this quarter I saw one of the perambulating cooks that of late years have become so rare in Paris. The cook was a woman in white apron, pushing a two-wheeled wagon before her, which bore a stove and a pile of uncooked sausages, and something known as *boudin,* flanked with a supply of bread. As she went along, she looked as vigilantly for customers as the driver of a Broadway stage, and cried "Sausages, fresh and cooked to order, all hot," with a peculiar intonation, for every perambulating merchant has each his or her peculiar cry. To a hungry man there was a savory smell from her viands, which produced its natural effect on several men in blouse near by, and induced an immediate outlay.

The perambulating cook of this kind of late years has become stationary, taken a shop, and extended the business, the poorer class of workmen being the chief clients. The hours of the working people — especially the women — have become longer, and there is less time to prepare more wholesome food. After a long day's work the woman often makes her repast of this seasoned meat, both from want of time and money. Fortunately, in this case, the Government has a hand in these pork preparations, in compelling, as far as it can, the purchase of sound meat; this mitigates the evils which might otherwise arise from the large consumption.

Among the poorest and most untidy of the poor women of Paris, is the *marchande des quatre saisons,* thus called because she sells the products of the four seasons, in the way of fruit and vegetables. Their traffic is not carried on in the poor quarters, but they lodge in them. One of them was wending her way home along the narrow street, endeavoring to dispose of the remnant of her wilted vegetables, as I passed. In a shrill tone and a familiar manner she addressed people at doors and windows, with her *cri de commerce,* and a running accompaniment as to the quality and cheapness of her products, which reminded me of Désaugiers's description: —

J'entends Javotte,
Portant sa hotte,
Crier: Carotte,
Panais et chou-fleur.
Perçant et grèle,
Son cri se mèle
A la frèle
Du noir ramoneur.

She *auctioneered* diligently, but with different results, for she was in a quarter where money was scarce. She appealed to possible customers in such familiar terms as "mon vieux," "ma biche," and "la petite mère," which was not taken amiss, for she was in a quarter, too, where people do not stand on ceremony.

In the neighborhood was the establishment of Mother Maillard, who sells the kind of nourishment called *arlequins,* already referred to. The Mother Maillard, it appears, has business relations with the scullions of several restaurants, from whom she buys the remains gathered from plates —not from the central, but those from which people eat. These bits of food are called *rogatons,* and are sold by the quantity, at so much a *seau.* With these the mother composes and cooks her arlequins. The usual price of this *olla podrida* is four frans a seau. A portion of the arlequins is sold as food for domestic animals and the remainder to the poor, she arranging each according to the required taste of man or animal. Many a Lazarus is fed in this way.

When her attention is called to the food hanging in her window, with the remark that that at least looks eatable, she replies that those things are only for show. On being further questioned she explains that the quarters of beef and mutton, usually seen in the windows of cheap soup-houses, are hired for the occasion to attract customers, and are returned to the butcher on demand.

Nothing is lost in the way of food in Paris, and the bones pass through several hands. First, the butcher sells them to the superior restaurant-keepers, who use them to make *bouillon,* and in the primitive state the butcher calls them collectively *réjouissance.* From the superior restaurants they pass to those of low grade at a considerable reduction, where they are again used to make soup. After this, the bones are handed over to the *gargotiers,* the lowest kind of eating-house keepers, where they again serve to make soup, with a miscellaneous mixture of carrots, onions, and odds and ends of different kinds. A spoonful of fish-oil thrown into the pot produces those little bubbles affectioned by the client, and gives the name to this liquid, *aux yeux de bouillon.* The mother admits that this has not an agreeable taste to the palate not accustomed to it, but thinks the taste must be acquired, like that for oysters, tomatoes, and tobacco.

In an old civilization every cranny and corner of public wants is filled. A crowd of poor men are always ready to take advantage of any opening of this kind to make a livelihood. One of the curious professions is that of a canary bird teacher, where the bird is taught to sing. Most of his time is occupied in training birds to sing, in his lodgings; but he also gives lessons in the town if required. The ordinary bird costs three francs, but when it has received its education its value is quadrupled. Should it turn out to be a *rara avis, —* say the Patti of canary birds, — the price becomes difficult to fix. Owners of birds often send them for a time to school to this professor to finish their education. For developing the musical faculties of the feathery pupil, a charge of five francs is made. There are probably more amateurs of these songsters here than elsewhere; hence the existence of such a singular calling. Most of us have been made familiar with the canary bird, as the natural complement of the *grisette* in the works of Sue and Béranger. The little warbler furnishes one of the consolations of life to many a solitary inhabitant of the mansard. In Mouffetard

Street an ancient ragpicker had turned bird-teacher, finding it more profitable than carrying the basket.

The pastimes of the poor run in little grooves. The cat is looked after, the canary bird is fed with care, and, if there is a child in this abode in miniature, it is cozened and kissed a dozen times a day. A pot or two of flowers at the one window are attended with daily solicitude; and these flowers often stimulate the little bourgeois to aspirations for the country, and he passes a good portion of his time in dreaming of green fields, running brooks, and village innocence. Then, if after twenty years of work and economy he gets money enough together, he buys one of those little white cottages with green Venetian shutters, so common in the villages around Paris. Here he devotes himself to his garden, in straw hat and blouse. The dreams of twenty years are realized, and two to one he is not happy; he finds himself regretting his narrow street and his dingy little shop, his dominoes, his café, and the habits of his quarter, and the chances are that he returns to them. He only finds repose in the noise of his old haunts. Here, in short, is a case where habit conquers nature.

In an open space of the Ménilmontant Quarter an animated scene presents itself every Sunday, which would make the hair of many of our sombre Puritans curl were they to see it. Revolving swings carry men and their sweethearts briskly up and down. Wooden horses on great wheels bear women and children whose faces are bright with pleasure. On platforms in front of rude little theatres, the whole company of each disports itself to attract visitors; the woman in short skirts of faded silk, with nude shoulders, at intervals beats the bass drum; the heavy man or *matamore* shows his brawny limbs in his most attractive *poses;* the Turlupin of the hour — the buffoon in old finery and rusty spangles — struts, twists, and turns, to the delight of the blouse- folk, as he cries out, "Walk in, ladies and gentlemen, there was never anything like it for the money: the drama of 'The Bloody Fiend;'

real sword fighting and killing on the stage; the Fat Woman weighing four hundred and fifty pounds, — a mountain of flesh, *quoi!* — in extraordinary contrast with the Living Skeleton, who will stand alongside of her; the Dancing Dog, who has danced before all the crowned heads of Europe, to say nothing of the President of the libre Amérique, — walk in," &c.; each harangue being followed by a few notes from a wheezy clarionet, and the boom, boom, of the bass drum.

A lemonade peddler with machine of shining brass strapped on his back, goblets attached to his shoulders, and bell in hand, circulates here and there, making his presence known with the cry of his craft.

Here too is the woman called the *marchande de plaisir,* peddling the hollow, fragile, cylindrical cakes known as *plaisirs,* dear to the mouth of women and children, with a similar cry.

There is also the gingerbread woman, jocularly termed by blouse people *"maman Pain-d'èpice,"* her name indicating the staple of her trade. Her line of operations, however, is not confined to this, for on her round turning lottery table are displayed macarons and croquets. The game of chance is an additional bait to her business, and she cries out at intervals, "D'excellents cr-r-r-r-oquets — à tout coup l'on gagne — approchez, approchez."

The majority of the crowd is composed of ragpickers, but here and there are people something higher in the social scale. Of these, a mother and her boy approach the table near which I am standing. It is covered with cakes, and I overhear the conversation as they draw near. "Well, my little man, what will you have, the macaroni cat or a gingerbread horse?" The boy devours the table with his eyes, but is mute. "Come, Paul," says the mother, "what will you have?" Paul's eyes take in the contents of the table, and he answers that he will take them all. Being, however, of an accommodating nature, he runs his chances, turns, and is obliged to choose between a mint-stick and a gingerbread sword. At length his warrior instincts, joined to a natural inclination toward gingerbread, prevail, and he draws the sword. The vender pronounces those amiable words, which are never wanting in the mouths of those who sell in France: "Madame, your son has the taste of a soldier; it is a good omen; he will one day be decorated." This flattery bears fruit, and the mother allows Paul to turn again, when he becomes the owner of a gingerbread heart, at which his eyes shine with a radiance that belongs only to childhood. It is another omen, and the mother is pleased. The heart and the sword! This is an epitome of a complete life in France,— love and glory.

The ragpickers may be regarded as the poorest poor of Paris. There is no other class of men whose lives are so narrow and so destitute as theirs. Several efforts were made in former times to break up their organization and do away with their occupation, but without success. They held to their rags as if they were purple and fine linen, and to their sorry food as if it were the nourishment of the Café Anglais. They will probably continue to cling to their misery with the tenacity of the past, until they receive, if they ever do, some sort of instruction from the State.

THE END.

Index